IN SEARCH OF THE
CREATION
FORMULA

The Art and Science of
Intentional Transformation

Nathan B. Jensen

In Search of The Creation Formula
The Art and Science of Intentional Transformation

Copyright © 2025 by Nathan B. Jensen

All rights reserved. No part of this book may be reproduced, distributed, or transmitted in any form or by any means, including photocopying, recording, or other electronic or mechanical methods, without the prior written permission of the author, except in the case of brief quotations embodied in critical reviews and certain other noncommercial uses permitted by copyright law.

The moral right of Nathan B. Jensen, as the author of this work, has been asserted in accordance with the Copyright, Designs, and Patents Act of 1988.

First Edition: 2025

DISCLAIMER

The information provided in this book is for educational and informational purposes only. They are not substitutes for professional medical, psychological, or therapeutic advice, diagnosis, or treatment. The author is not a licensed medical professional or therapist, and the information contained in this book should not be interpreted as medical, financial, or psychological advice.

Before implementing any changes or strategies discussed in this book, especially those related to mental, emotional, or physical health, consult a licensed healthcare professional to determine what may be best for your needs. The author assumes no responsibility for any errors, omissions, or liability for any adverse effects, losses, or damages caused directly or indirectly by using any information in this book.

The techniques, exercises, and suggestions are based on the author's experiences and research. Results may vary, and success is not guaranteed. The responsibility for applying the ideas and practices in this book rests entirely with the reader.

Any references to individuals, organizations, or specific events are purely for illustrative purposes and should not be taken as endorsements or slights. Any perceived slights to individuals or entities are entirely unintentional.

CONTENTS

Introduction 1

Phase 1: Expand 17

Wake Up: Stop Lying About Reality! 27

Awareness: The Key to Transformation 35

Acceptance: Stop Fighting What Is 43

Ownership: Take Responsibility 51

The Frame: Defining the "Lens" of Reality 59

The Reframe: Seeing Life with New Eyes 63

Rewriting Your Stories 71

Transformation: Embracing the Path to Expand 78

Phase 2: Elevate 83

The Four Pillars of a Balanced Life 95

System Thinking Versus Linear Thinking 99

Habits That Build The Four Pillars 103

Elevate The Pillar of Vitality 107

Elevate The Pillar of Insight 110

Elevate The Pillar of Harmony 116

Elevate The Pillar of Purpose 120

Start a Powerful Day 123

The Journey of Elevation 126

Phase 3: Envision 129

Looking Forward to the Future 132

Crafting a Crystal-Clear Vision 138

Dreaming Big, Creating Bigger 143

Moving Across the Gap 150

Focusing On the Gain 154

Harnessing Your Creative Force 163

Stepping Forward with Faith 168

Closing the Loop: From Vision to Reality 174

Conclusion 177

References 180

About The Author 184

INTRODUCTION

On October 10, 2011, I found myself sitting in the hospital waiting room, feeling the anxiety slowly rising within me. It had been a few hours since I kissed my wife, Amy, goodbye and whispered that I loved her. Helplessly, I stood there as they wheeled her into the operating room, wishing I could have held her just a little longer. Now, I sat in the waiting room, bracing myself for the long hours ahead, anxiously awaiting the results of her surgery.

During our preliminary doctor visits, the doctor casually referred to it as a "piece of cake" brain surgery, assuring us that Amy would be home recovering in no time. Although the medical team didn't believe it was cancer, the urgency of the surgery was apparent. The tumor, lodged against her pituitary gland and pressing on the optic nerve, was already causing Amy to lose her vision.

Finally, after several nerve-racking hours, the surgeon came into our waiting room, where he was surprised by the number of people waiting for the excellent news that Amy's surgery had gone well and that she was

Introduction

recovering. With trepidation, he delivered the news that the surgery had some complications. He told me that when the tumor was being biopsied, it hemorrhaged, and she lost massive amounts of blood. By the time they could stop the bleeding and give her the needed blood transfusion, her brain had been without adequate blood flow for nearly twenty minutes, and he didn't know if she would recover. The news hit me like the weight of a ton of bricks.

As my family and I made it up to the ICU to see Amy, we were stopped and told to wait again in the waiting area. Finally, after another couple of hours, we were brought back to see her, and at that time, we were given even more difficult news that Amy had two massive strokes in the ICU. They had done some brain scans, and the brain had very little activity. The doctor and staff advised us that the outlook was not good.

I stood by Amy's bedside in shock and disbelief that this was happening to me and my family. I was so incredibly sick to my stomach. I stood there and prayed my heart out to God for that miracle that he might grant unto me that Amy could recover and be healed from all of this. It was 3 a.m. when her father, Ed, came into the room to relieve me and told me to go lie down for a few minutes while he would stay with Amy. I went and found a couch in the waiting area and tried to stretch out to relieve my aching back. I could feel the pain everywhere in my body, including the sick pit in my stomach that sat there gnawing at me. I couldn't sleep, but I closed my eyes, trying to process what was happening to me.

After an hour, I returned to Amy's room to find Ed sitting by her side, and he told me that when I left the room, Amy's countenance had a subtle change. I could see the change, too, but while on life support, we were still unsure until the morning when tests were run that showed the brain had ceased to function. Then Ed and I looked at each other, and we knew it was during that early hour in the morning that Amy's spirit left her broken body and passed on.

The weight of pain and anguish was overwhelming at that moment, and one of the most challenging experiences of my life was telling my children, as we stood by her bedside, that their mother had passed away. We shed countless tears that day and for many months after. Even now, years later, as I write this, I can still feel the heaviness of that day and the deep sorrow that followed.

The deep pain and anguish lingered for many months, but as the weight gradually lifted, I began the journey of rebuilding my life. Pain and hardship were not new to me. At twenty-seven, I went through a difficult divorce, during which I was homeless for a time with my two young children. After gaining custody, I moved to Utah, returned to school, and earned my degree in electrical engineering with minors in physics and math. A year after graduating, I met Amy. We married, and together, we blended our tiny families.

A couple of years later, my closest and dearest friend, Joe Wheeler, took his life one day after he and his wife were struggling with marital issues. And then, almost a

Introduction

year later, at a family reunion, our nearly three-year-old daughter Samantha was killed by a rock that came tumbling off the nearby mountain slope. These are the stories that shape our lives.

The things that happen to us after tragedies strike define us and the lives of those around us. After my first divorce, I was able to bounce back and recreate a positive, hopeful future. Was it because I was young and had a lot to look forward to, or was it because I could spin the past trauma into something positive? These are some of the things we will explore later in this book.

When my friend Joe took his own life, it left me feeling deeply depressed, haunted by the thought that maybe I could have done more to support him. Yet, even in hindsight, there were no clear signs that he was struggling to the extent he was. His actions shocked everyone. That experience ignited a strong desire to uplift those around me and be more present for others in their times of need.

With my daughter's accident, my wife Amy taught me a lot about accepting "what is" in life. She mourned profoundly but was an inspiration to me and many others for the love and kindness she would show to complete strangers. On one occasion, Amy ran into a grieving couple that had just lost their young son. She was a budding photographer and was very experienced with Photoshop. Whenever she found a family that had lost a child or loved one, she offered to photoshop the loved one into their new family photo.

Amy seemed to process her grief by blessing the lives of others who were suffering a similar tragedy.

During the years between Samantha's death and Amy's, I worked hard to be a good dad to my children and maintain my software development job. I was good at my job, but life wore on me, and I felt deep dark depression for many years. I took every possible antidepressant drug combination to overcome it and even had my DNA tested for the best possible combination that would help me. I thought this was just who I was and that I would suffer from depression for the rest of my life. I didn't know that it would be possible to overcome it and that perhaps I was creating the very depression that was debilitating me over time.

I am relatively sure that if you were to share the same experiences with your doctor, they would do something similar and put you on some medication, too. Although I do believe there is a place for medication and it can help, I was then left to keep thinking, feeling, and doing the same things over and over in my life that would perpetuate the same results of depression. As I discovered through my journey in life, you, too, will find out in the chapters that follow how to combat and overcome the mental and emotional traps that can exaggerate or solve the problem. You will also discover how you are the creator of your life. You will find the power to make incredible changes intentionally and rapidly that affect The Four Pillars of your life.

Introduction

Now, back to my journey. A little over a year after Amy's passing, I remarried a widow who had lost her husband in a motorcycle accident. Many family members were concerned that I was rushing into things, and probably rightly so because nine months later, I was facing a divorce. I kept trying to make it work for another few months until neither of us wanted to try anymore. The papers were signed, and we both moved on.

The divorce reopened the painful wounds of the past and restoked the flames of my grief from the death of Amy. The pain was very evident in my everyday life, and all I wanted to do was escape it.

That same year, my mother passed away at the age of seventy-two after suffering from liver cancer. She was always there for me during those hard years, especially after Amy's death. She was there to listen to me when I needed a listening ear and someone to encourage me. And now she was gone.

Before my mother passed, I once turned to my father for comfort after my wife's death, only to be told to "get over it." Now, he was facing that same heartbreak I had known all too well. Understanding what he was likely going through, I made it a point to call him often, trying to offer some comfort. I could hear the familiar pain in his voice.

Isn't it interesting that we often have many opinions and expectations on how people should live until we experience something similar?

Then we begin to see life through a whole different set of lenses. This new perspective can help us be empathetic witnesses to other people and can create rapid transformation in our own lives. In later chapters of this book, you will discover exciting ways to define and use perspective as you build out a new vision for your life.

The following year, I spent recovering and recuperating, trying to reinvent my life once again. Each traumatic experience in my life forced a change in my life, whether I wanted it or not. I was forced to face it and decide what I should do. Many times, I didn't handle it well, and if I hadn't been brought up in a strong religious family, I may have chosen to sedate my pain in ways that would have left me a lot worse off.

I can see how easy it is for people to choose paths of sedation that include drugs and alcohol because the pain is tremendous, and so often, we want it to stop. This is another concept we will discuss in how to turn our pain into power and how to stop sedating our feelings. When we sedate ourselves, we limit our ability to create the life we want, which is the recipe for staying stuck in life. You will discover the power to put away the sedation, and once removed, it will open the door to new possibilities that you never thought were possible.

After feeling that I had spent enough time healing from Amy's death and my recent divorce, I decided to try again with a new relationship. This time, I remarried a

Introduction

divorcee who had never experienced widowhood. Little did I realize the turmoil my late wife's memory would stir in her mind. It wasn't until my son found a broken and discarded photo of his mother in the trash that I fully grasped the emotional toll it was taking on her.

My struggle in this new relationship was beyond anything I had experienced before. But in this relationship, I discovered how people see the world and formulate their reality. Although our eyes can deliver the bits of data to our brain in the same way, it's our brain that interprets the data, and that is why no two witnesses of an accident will report the same events occurring in the same way even if they are standing in the same spot and viewing it from the same direction. It's because the way our brains work is individual, and how we process the data is unique to each of us.

Simply put, she had a way of viewing life as if it were always working against her. She constantly believed I desired someone else, and it became impossible for us to go anywhere in public without it becoming a confrontation. I sought therapy and marriage counseling, but counseling rarely works when you walk in believing the other person is the problem. So I chose to approach it as though I needed change, and from there, I began the most profound transformational journey of my life.

My transformation began while I was still in the relationship, enduring constant verbal attacks until I reached my emotional breaking point, which ultimately led to our divorce. One day, I came across something that changed my perspective—it said that those who are mentally and emotionally healthy wouldn't tolerate such abuse for even a single day, let alone a minute. That's when it hit me: I wasn't as mentally and emotionally healthy as I thought. So I removed myself from the toxic situation and continued my quest for the "how-to" of building a fulfilling and purposeful life.

Over the next several years, I immersed myself in personal development, enrolling in course after course from some of the most influential leaders in the field. I developed a daily habit of reading, working through several hundred of the best books, and journaling through past traumas. I also participated in various mentoring and coaching programs. Along the way, I became certified in NLP (Neuro-Linguistic Programming), meditation instruction, high-performance coaching, and hypnotherapy while exploring numerous other techniques and concepts. Learning has always been one of my superpowers, and my passion for neuroscience has fueled this journey for many years.

I have also adopted a new belief that "life happens for me" rather than "life happens to me." I can now use my past trauma as a tool to teach me what I need to know in life. Through all of it, I have discovered and learned from the most outstanding teachers and instructors of our time. I have taken and practiced some of the latest in neuroscience to transform my life. And I have formulated a three-phase approach to intentional

Introduction

transformation. I am a scientist by nature, so I call it The Creation Formula, and it looks something like this in mathematical notation.

$$E^3 = RT$$
or
(Expand * Elevate * Envision) = Rapid Transformation

This is a three-phase approach to achieving rapid transformation. If you've ever felt like giving up on life, suffered from poor health, been stuck or burned out in your career, or watched your relationships fall apart—and you're ready for a change—this book is for you. It is designed in three phases, and I will break down each phase. As you follow along and engage in the work for each phase, you will begin to see, feel, and experience profound and rapid transformation in your life.

Before I started my journey of discovering The Creation Formula, my life was in shambles, and my relationships were broken. Not only was I going through a divorce, but my relationships with my children were also broken and in need of repair. As for my career, I was barely hanging on by a thread, doing the bare minimum to maintain my job.

In my search and journey of discovering The Creation Formula, I have been able to break away from the negative self-defeating stories of my past. I have recreated myself repeatedly in body, mind, and spirit to the point that life is what I create, and I can say life is great again.

In Search of The Creation Formula

I am free from depression and anxiety that used to stick to me like glue. I feel more joy, happiness, and freedom than I have ever experienced. My relationships are repaired with my children, and I have been able to be there for them as they go through their own trials.

I was able to attract Janice, a beautiful, kind, and loving woman, into my life. We met at a dance class that we both felt inspired to attend and from our very first date, I could tell she was heaven-sent. She has been the perfect match for me. Our relationship has been one of the easiest I have ever had.

Janice, too, has had a similar story of losing her spouse unexpectedly and then remarrying someone who was utterly incompatible with her. Still, her journey in life led her to me and mine to her, and I couldn't be happier.

There are still complex challenges that we face together of blending a family and helping our children mend from the traumatic experiences that they had from losing a parent and the other experiences of being dragged through relationships that failed in divorce. I now have the knowledge, the tools, and the ability to bless our children's lives and help them feel loved and appreciated.

My career, too, transformed in unique ways. What used to be a tedious and dead-end job turned into a captivating challenge. I raised myself to a new standard and achieved the highest possible exceptional rating. I also became a leader and a coach to engineers, helping them become high performers—not just in their careers but in life.

Introduction

To reach and maintain a high-performance status in life and stay consistently at that level without burning out over time, you must understand the formula that will get you there and keep you there. The key is to put the three phases of Expand, Elevate, and Envision into practice.

Living by The Creation Formula transforms life rapidly into the life you want. Happiness, joy, and fulfillment are merely the "fruits" of this formula.

The Creation Formula

The initial starting point for The Creation Formula came when I was having lunch with my oldest son. I can remember quite vividly the day it all started. I was sitting there sharing with him how miserable my life had been and how hopeless and stuck I felt in life. And after a few minutes, I could see his frustration with me start to reach a boiling point, and he looked at me and forcefully said, "Dad, stop being a victim!" His words were like a sharp knife that cut me to the core. It sent a shock wave of pain throughout my body. I was not expecting that reaction at all.

> *"And ye shall know the truth, and the truth shall make you free."*
> **– John 8:32**

I sat with those words of "Stop being a victim" for a long time, many days, in fact. I questioned myself, "Am I being a victim?" and "How am I being a victim?" What does it even mean to be a victim? As I progressed through my journey of transformation over the next few years, growing and becoming a new version of myself over and over, I spent a considerable amount of time studying and contemplating what it meant to be a victim and what it would mean to be the creator of my own life.

The biggest revelation that came to me was that victims carry the mindset that life happens to them. The result of this mindset means that you have no control over your life. Your life is controlled by your circumstances and the environment you live in. There is no way out, and it's everyone's fault that you feel like you do. This leaves no room for change and prevents you from being able to be the creator of your life.

This is the world we live in now. Just look around. Everywhere you look in the media, someone is blaming someone else for why they are depressed or suppressed. If you don't recognize who they are or what pronoun to use, they are offended. It's someone else's fault because they can't get into college, get a job, find someone to love or succeed in life. Everyone wants to think and be whoever or whatever they want, but when you don't accept their insanity or have a contrary opinion about it, they get offended and blame you for their pain and suffering.

Once you start to understand and pay attention to the victim mentality, you will see it everywhere. This world needs more creators as leaders and teachers. With more people learning to take responsibility for what they think, feel, and do, we would see a greater abundance of love, joy, and happiness spread throughout.

When you stop blaming others for your life, you can stop resenting them; when you stop resenting others, you can stop hating them. When you stop hating people, the door of possibility opens, and behind this door are unlimited possibilities. The door can now be opened to loving your neighbor and, most importantly, loving yourself.

What it means to be a creator is to take 100 percent responsibility for your life. The first level of being a creator operates with the mindset that life "happens for me" and "by me." The premise of the following formula is to provide a way for you to be the creator of your life.

$$E^3 = RT$$
(Expand * Elevate * Envision) = Rapid Transformation

In each phase of this equation, you will see the evidence and research that backs up each component. After spending over a decade learning the concepts and best practices of the various parts that comprise The Creation Formula, you will find it much easier to conceptualize the multiple components in the three phases of Expand, Elevate, and Envision. And rather than spending a decade learning and practicing the concepts you are about to learn in this book, your transformation can take place in ninety days or less.

As in basic math, you will learn how to take these three inputs and create the results you want in life. Whether it be improved relationships, excellent health and wellness, or more abundance of wealth, you will learn how to apply this formula to attract the things you want into your life like a magnet. You will discover how easy it can become to be the creator of a purpose-filled, rewarding, and fulfilling life.

Let's break down the formula into simple components and understand why they are essential to your transformational journey.

PHASE 1
EXPAND

> *"No problem can be solved from the same level of consciousness that created it."*
> **– Albert Einstein**

The big problem I faced in my life after I had gone through so much loss and failed relationships, along with a stagnant and boring career where I felt burned out all of the time, was that I felt trapped in a pit of despair. Was I destined to live a life full of pain, where nothing I did seemed to make it better? I felt like I was living the same day over and over again, much like in the movie *Groundhog Day*.

How was I ever going to break free from this cycle? Have you ever felt something similar stuck in your own life? Do recurring thoughts of failure bring you pain? Despite everything you've tried, do you get the same results repeatedly?

> "We don't see the world as it is,
> we see it as we are."
> **– Anaïs Nin**

Life In the Matrix

I am a big fan of the science fiction movie *The Matrix* (1999) because it paints this picture more vividly, where we are all asleep and living in this simulated reality. The film explores the nature of reality and human freedom. The story follows Thomas A. Anderson, Keanu Reeve's character, a computer programmer who leads a double life as the hacker Neo. He discovers he is living in a simulated reality known as the Matrix. Guided by Morpheus and Trinity, Neo learns to navigate and manipulate the Matrix, ultimately realizing his potential as "The One" destined to destroy the artificial intelligence enslaving human life.

The film explores some extremely thought-provoking themes of reality, perception, and freedom that can be so relatable to our own lives.

In a pivotal moment, Morpheus gives Neo a choice: "This is your last chance. After this, there is no turning back. You take the blue pill—the story ends, and you wake up in your bed and believe whatever you want to believe. You take the red pill—you stay in Wonderland, and I show you how deep the rabbit hole goes."

One of the most significant realizations that came about over several years was realizing that I was the one who was building my matrix, the prison that I felt myself trapped in. I built it stone by stone over the decades of living. I would say I wasn't consciously aware of building it or even aware of putting a single stone on any of the walls I built up over time. However, I later understood and realized that each stone was created by the programming I had received throughout my lifetime.

It's that eye-opening moment when we wake up and finally realize that our current reality is not what we perceive it to be. We discover that we have been living in this small, confined box constructed and decorated by our minds.

Would it be surprising to realize that you, too, are living in the Matrix?

Waking up to the truth is that our reality is just a construction of everything we have been taught to believe since birth. We are all living inside the reality that we have created. It is what we see through the "lens" of our vision of the world, and it defines what is happening all around us.

Our perception of reality is influenced by our reticular activation system (RAS), which acts as a filter or gatekeeper for information entering the brain. It filters out irrelevant or unnecessary information, allowing you to focus on what's important. It is your brain's natural filtering system.

Your subconscious programs can trigger this filter without our conscious mind even being aware, and this is what keeps us in the Matrix, oblivious to an accurate perception of reality.

This realization becomes a great awakening, where you can finally start to see life differently. Waking up to this fact allows you to question your programming, which will change the filter and "lens" from which you see life, resulting in liberation from the Matrix.

Thoughts Create Your Reality

All of our lives, from the time we were conceived and even up till now, our thoughts and beliefs have been shaped and conditioned by family, education, society, culture, religion, media, and even our genes (imprinted on us by sensory experiences of our lives and generational inheritance). We have been told what to think and how to think. Studies suggest a toddler is told "No" 400 to 500 times daily. You would get a "No" every ninety seconds. This isn't always bad, but do you see that the boundaries of life and limitations taught to us begin to formulate at a young age?

Our brain is designed to assess every experience we have in life and form a belief about it. The movie *Inside Out 2* perfectly portrays how our brain takes memory and formulates a belief. Each belief forms the rules and constructs of our internal operating system.

I was first exposed to the idea of limiting beliefs in the early 1990s through Tony Robbins's books and courses. In 1991, I made significant transformational changes in my life while struggling as a single father with two young children. When I was initially introduced to these ideas, I didn't fully understand how our past traumas and programming create our reality and define the "lens" through which we see life.

It wasn't until I came across Dr. Caroline Leaf, a neuroscientist specializing in psychoneurobiology and metacognitive neuropsychology, that I gained the understanding, power, and belief that I could change my brain and life. Dr. Leaf was one of the first in her field to study how the brain can change (neuroplasticity) with directed mind input. I have been passionate about learning about the brain for years, but reading her books fueled my passion even more.

A few years later, Dr. Joe Dispenza brought to light and full circle some of the ideas I had been learning about over the last decade. Here is one such powerful snippet. Ponder it for a moment.

"Your past shortfalls can be traced, at their root, to one major oversight: you haven't committed yourself to living by the truth that *your thoughts have consequences so great that they create your reality.*"

Your thoughts create your reality. At first, your brain might want to fight against that notion because your original belief might be that your circumstances create your reality. Almost everyone I speak to is convinced of the same thing, but they do it unconsciously because that is what we are taught to believe. How many arguments have you been in because you did something that made someone else angry?

Was it really what you said that made them angry, or was there a thought about what was said that produced the emotions?

Three Different Outcomes

Let's create a simple scenario where someone walks up to you and says, "You are such a jerk." I will define this circumstance as the facts.

Now, let's introduce a variable into the facts. The variable is the "someone," like a stranger, a friend, or a very close loved one.

How does your brain respond to this situation when the "someone" is a stranger? Perhaps something like, "Wow, that guy is crazy. He doesn't know what he is even talking about." You may or may not experience some emotions of anger or indifference and then go on about your day.

But let's say that "someone" is now your friend, and they say, "You are such a jerk." Your brain may produce a thought like: "Are they playing with me? Or do they mean it?" and several other thoughts might follow, producing some immediate defensiveness and other noticeable emotions and pain.

Finally, let's say the "someone" is much closer to you, like a spouse or partner, and they say, "You are such a jerk." What kind of thoughts will your brain produce, maybe something like: "What, did you just call me that? Why are you attacking me?" Immediately, your defensive shield is raised, and your mind begins to spin around what is happening. More noticeably, there will be some deeper emotions the body will feel, and the sharpness of the pain you might experience will be quite a bit more distinct.

Your suffering is directly proportional to the amount of meaning and belief that you give a thought.

When your subconscious mind compares the three scenarios, it will have been processing the situations of each quite differently, adding meaning without you even realizing it, producing the feelings that follow the verbal attack.

The closer the individual is to you, the more meaning your mind will give to the experience, and the thoughts generated in your brain will be different.

The more you believe the thoughts and the deeper the meaning you give them, the greater the emotions produced in the body.

Your reality is a by-product of what you think and feel rather than the situation itself, and then, based on what you think, there is an action. You argue, fight back, with insulting comments of your own, or perhaps you ignore it.

Given any of the three scenarios, what if, just for a moment, you did not believe the words? What if you were able to attach zero meaning to the situation? Then what emotions would be elicited in you? You would have a completely different experience, wouldn't you? And because of this new experience you created, how would your reality be different?

Ghosted Again

Here is another scenario: You just texted a group of friends about an upcoming event to which you have invited them and asked, "Who would like to go?" No one responded.

After a few minutes, what thoughts start to pass through your mind? What are they after an hour? How about after twenty-four hours without a single response?

Every thought formed in the brain creates a chemical reaction. As the thoughts get worse, so are the feelings that they make. Your old story that "No one cares about me" pops up in your mind.

This old story already has some deep negative emotions associated with it. This story is about an existing program running in your subconscious mind, installed there from some experience from your past. It is now processing the data and has confirmed the validity of your old story with newfound evidence to support it; this is called confirmation bias. With this evidence, you will take action and decide from here on out that you will not invite these friends to any more activities with you.

What is the reality that you have created for yourself?

Your brain doesn't question its validity because it has a built-in filtering system that accepts or rejects data based on your current programming.

It doesn't matter if there are other facts that support the opposite version of the story you are telling yourself. Those facts are discarded. This processing that our brain goes through defines the "lens" from which we see reality. An original thought starts this whole process, and with some confirmation bias, a story or program is written in your subconscious mind. We begin to build our matrix with a set of programs that control how we see the world.

What if you were to begin to expand and break free from your current reality?

> *"I'm trying to free your mind, Neo. But I can only show you the door.*
> *You're the one that has to walk through it."*
> **– Morpheus**

By questioning the validity of the old stories that come to light over time, your "lens" of reality will start seeing new facts and interesting data previously discarded.

Phase 1: Expand

Only when you question your current stories and expand your consciousness can you open the door to new possibilities and move beyond your current limitations.

By expanding your consciousness, you can break free from restrictive beliefs, habits, and patterns that hinder personal growth and transformation. It is where you can tear down the prison walls you have built for yourself and create the life you want. Expansion can be a new reality, one that is entirely different from the one in which you currently reside.

This section will guide you through concepts designed to challenge and change your programming. These concepts will ultimately teach you how to shift from a victim to a creator mindset, allowing you to redesign your current reality.

Transformation is just one expansion away.

WAKE UP

STOP LYING ABOUT REALITY!

> *"Until you make the unconscious conscious, it will direct your life, and you will call it fate."*
> **– Carl Jung**

The great awakening came for me the day I was told I was a victim. It caused me deep reflection and much internal pain. Because of this, I later signed up for a personal development conference where I had the experience of a guy screaming directly into my face, "You are a liar!" It was a bit shocking. Yet, sometimes, it does take such an event in life to wake us up from the false reality that we are living.

Is it possible that you are living life with a victim mindset?

Waking up is the opening up to the realization that you can be the creator of the current life you are living. You can be the creator of your reality. It is possible to do things that you used to think were impossible. To create the life you desire, you must uncover the programming that has been keeping you imprisoned.

When the guy at the conference screamed in my face that I was a liar, he was trying to impress upon me that I had been lying to myself for years. I have been crafting excuses for why I am the way I am for so long that they have become my identity and personality.

In what areas of your life have you been making excuses to justify who you are or how you live?

Let me share a couple of simple examples of lies that have kept me stuck for a long time.

Lie #1: I am a night person

Have you ever heard someone say they can't get up early because they are a night person? For most of my adult life, I believed I was a night person and would tell people there was no way I was a morning person. I would avoid getting up early and work or game late into the night, sometimes into the early morning, going to bed exhausted and sleeping late.

The next day, I would drag myself out of bed late and arrive at work with my forty-four-ounce Diet Dr. Pepper, or one of my favorite RockStar energy drinks. I would chug down the caffeine to wake myself up, all in vain, so I could live life running half-empty.

It didn't matter that at eight years old, my father started my brothers and me working in the family business, and he would get us up at 5:30 in the morning. We'd go to work for a couple of hours before school every morning. We did this through our teenage years, day in and day out. Could that be where my mind created the program that I hated to get up early? Let's be honest. I did hate it.

It wasn't until I became aware of what I was telling myself about being a night person that I could see the results of the lie and what it was creating in my life. The consistent negative results helped me finally address the lie. It wasn't true what I was telling myself; the lie only kept me stuck in my old patterns of living.

> *"Men go through life trying to change the circumstances of their life, blind to the fact that the circumstances that they seek to change were the creations of their own minds."*
> – Neville Goddard

Once, **I told myself**, "I can be a morning person," **and I believed it.** That is when the shift occurred, and things began to change. I was able to create new habits. I got some newfound rest and deeper sleep. What amazed me most was seeing how just one small change could affect so many areas of my life.

Lie #2: I am a depressed person, it's just in my DNA

Another lie I had told myself for years was that I was convinced my depression was just who I was. I would wake up in the morning feeling the depression just weighing on me like a heavy-weight blanket. I could not break free from it. I was convinced it was genetic and had sought many treatments and drugs with very little help.

It wasn't until I questioned my thoughts about my depression that an article stood out about how exercise was more effective at helping depression than antidepressants. The study showed how the body, due to exercise, creates endorphins, dopamine, serotonin, and other proteins, which can be more powerful and better than anything that could be prescribed. A simple search will provide hundreds of articles with these facts, and I think most of us have heard of the benefits of exercise.

If we know about it, why doesn't it create change in us?

I had seen articles like this before, but remember the "lens" through which we see reality—it filters out the facts that won't support it. I can only see what my programming wants me to see. If I don't believe exercise is effective, I won't consider it. I will ignore all the facts that would support it. However, what finally creates a change in your limiting beliefs is when you start to question them.

In Search of The Creation Formula

I remember the day when I was so tired of the side effects of the drugs I was on that I decided that perhaps exercise could work, and I set a tiny goal, one that would be easy to do. My goal was simple: just put on my gym clothes and walk through the gym doors every day. It wasn't to work out hard or anything like that, but it was merely to walk through those gym doors. I knew that once I got myself there, I would do something. I started with a few minutes of walking on the treadmill, and progressively, over a few months, I added more cardio and weightlifting.

It's now been several years, and I am free from any antidepressant drug. And the best thing about it is I feel alive and healthy again, without the nasty side effects of those antidepressants. This slight shift in questioning a single belief has transformed my life. Improved health and mood have affected my body, mind, spirit, relationships, and income.

The tiny shift in believing that exercise could be the answer completely transformed my life and created a new reality.

Here is a "tiny" list of common lies people tell themselves daily:

- I am not good enough.
- I am not worthy of love/success/happiness.
- I am not pretty enough.
- I am too short.
- I can't change.
- I'm too old to go back to school.
- I'm too young to apply for that job.

- I always fail, so why even try?
- It needs to be perfect.
- People will judge me.
- I can't afford it.
- It's too late to start.
- I don't have the right connections.
- I am an introvert/extrovert.
- I am not a morning person or night person.
- I can't save money.
- I don't make enough to save.
- Opportunities always pass me by.
- I am too tired to exercise.
- No one cares about me.
- No one likes me.

I say "tiny" because once you begin the journey of awareness, you will discover this list can get very long, very fast.

Just the Facts

So you don't have someone screaming in your face to wake up and stop lying about your life. I don't think I will do that to you, but I have found a much simpler approach.

We must start with the facts to uncover the bugs in our programming. Where are you in all areas of your life right now? Being honest about where you are is key to transformation.

By identifying the facts in your life, you weed out the judgments you may have inadvertently created around them. When you start processing the facts about your life, you will begin to uncover the malware installed in your programming that has kept you stuck or broken. Armed with the facts, you will have a good baseline from which you can start your journey of intentional transformation and creating the life of your dreams.

Action

Pull out a notebook or journal, and let's begin by creating three columns. In one column, we want to identify all the facts currently surrounding these critical areas of your life.

Body (Health and Fitness)
Well-being (Mental/Emotional/Spiritual)
Relationships (Spouse/Partner/Children/Friends)
Income (Business/Career/Investments)

Be sure you get as detailed as possible in each vital area. A fact usually can be measured, but in the area of well-being, it can be a little less subjective. In relationships, you may have to ask someone to rate you on how well they believe your relationship with them is so that you can create a baseline from which you can work.

An example of your body and health might be: I currently weigh 225 pounds, my waist size is 42, my shirt size is XL, I am on high blood pressure pills, etc.

An example of well-being is that I pray once a week, go to church every month, and read one book a month.

My happiness level is five out of ten, and my spiritual connectedness is four out of ten.

An example of income: I make $90,000 a year, I save $300 a month, and I have $5,000 saved.

An example of a career: I am currently a project manager.

An example of a business: I currently own and operate Big Belly Burger, which has gross revenues of $100,000 monthly and a net income of $40,000 monthly.

Once you have written down all the areas you care about, then in the next column, you will want to put down what the ideal would look like. Here is the critical step: when you write down what you see or believe the ideal should be, notice the thought that comes up about the ideal and write it down in the third column. This thought is often the program that keeps you stuck in the matrix and away from what you want.

Note: Get book bonuses, where you can complete a comprehensive assessment for each key area of your life or download a copy for your personal use. For book bonuses, go to: e3blueprint.com/bookbonus

AWARENESS

THE KEY TO TRANSFORMATION

> *"Awareness is like the sun. When it shines on things, they are transformed."*
> **– Thich Nhat Hanh**

The wake-up call to stop being the victim and to be the creator of your life awakens this little-known muscle of awareness within you. For it to grow, it must be exercised, and just like any muscle in your body, if you don't use it, it will weaken and eventually atrophy. With greater awareness, we can discover limiting programming that has kept us stuck for years. When we neglect to exercise our awareness—when we stop paying attention to our thoughts, emotions, and the world around us—we start to lose touch with reality.

The Key to Transformation

This loss of awareness can trap us in a mentally and emotionally fabricated reality where our limiting beliefs, fears, and external influences control us. In this place, we operate on autopilot, reacting to life rather than consciously living it. We become prisoners of our minds, unable to see beyond the illusions we've accepted as truth.

We must actively engage and strengthen our awareness muscles to escape this false reality and regain control of our lives. This means practicing mindfulness, challenging our assumptions, and being present in each moment. Just as physical exercise keeps our bodies healthy and robust, mental exercise through awareness keeps our minds sharp and accessible. By doing so, we break free from the constraints of our false reality and reclaim our power to create a new, beautiful life of purpose and fulfillment.

My late wife was a photographer, so I bought these expensive camera lenses for her photography business. One was a telephoto lens, while the other was a wide-angle lens. A wide-angle lens has a shorter focal length than a standard lens, and photographers use it to expand the horizontal scope of the camera shot, with subjects closer to the camera appearing more prominent than subjects farther away. The telephoto lens is a long-focus lens that allows photographers to focus on a single (often faraway) subject and create contrast between the foreground and the background.

Awareness is like having both wide-angle and telephoto lenses in your mental toolkit. Just as Amy used a wide-angle lens to capture a broad scene, awareness allows us to take in the bigger picture of our lives, seeing all aspects clearly and understanding how different elements are interconnected. With its ability to focus on distant subjects and bring them into sharp relief, the telephoto lens mirrors how awareness helps us zero in on specific thoughts or emotions, understanding their impact and significance amid the broader context of our experiences.

Mindfulness

Mindfulness is the practice that enables us to switch between these two lenses with ease. It teaches us to be present in the moment, fully experiencing and acknowledging our thoughts, feelings, and surroundings without judgment. Just as my wife needed both lenses to capture the full spectrum of a scene, we need mindfulness to balance our awareness, helping us see the vast panorama of our lives while honing in on the finer details. By cultivating mindfulness, we become more adept at shifting our focus, allowing us to create the reality we desire and navigate it with greater clarity and insight.

Mindfulness was a foreign concept to me, but I had heard about meditation for years. I had often thought that I should try it out, so one day, I called a friend and asked him if he wanted to take a meditation class with me.

The Key to Transformation

Arriving at the class, we were directed to sit on a nearby mat with a pillow. I looked around to see what others were doing and tried to fit in. Our meditation instructor began with a gong of his meditation bell. He spoke softly and calmly and walked us through our first mindfulness meditation.

The experience was calming and different enough that I wanted to learn more. So I spent the next year learning everything I could about meditation and its mental and health benefits. Mindfulness is a practice of being fully present and engaged in the current moment, aware of your thoughts, feelings, and sensations without judgment. It involves paying attention, on purpose, to the present moment and cultivating an attitude of openness and acceptance toward whatever arises.

There has been a lot of talk lately about mindfulness, and it is needed more than ever in our fast-paced world. We are so distracted by our electronic devices, and our focus and attention are being pulled in so many directions simultaneously, leaving our brains overwhelmed and exhausted. This constant state of distraction prevents us from truly experiencing the present moment, leading to increased stress, anxiety, and a sense of disconnection from ourselves and others.

Mindfulness remedies this modern dilemma by teaching us to slow down, breathe, and return our attention to the here and now. It allows us to experience the present moment.

The experience of the present moment is quite simply what remains when no thought arises in our minds or we don't engage in the action of believing a thought.

Practicing mindfulness can reclaim mental clarity, reduce stress levels, and foster a deeper sense of peace and well-being. It allows us to step out of the autopilot mode of living and engage with life more fully and intentionally. Mindfulness is the deliberate application of our awareness. It allows us to cut through the noise and chaos of our fast-paced lives and helps us to find balance, focus, and a more profound connection to the world around us.

Remember the RAS, the part of the brain that filters incoming data? Mindfulness will fine-tune the RAS with greater attention and focus. This will be critically important when reprogramming an old story and creating a new one. You will want your mind to collect data to support your new story so the programming you want to support sticks.

One of the most important and overlooked aspects of practicing awareness is becoming aware of your emotional triggers and responses. In the Cognitive Behavioral Therapy CBT (think, feel, and do) model, thoughts create feelings, feelings create behavior in us, and our behavior reinforces the thought. This creates a continuous cycle of how thoughts influence our emotions, leading to actions that, in turn, affect thoughts, creating a constant cycle. A greater awareness of this cycle will help you uncover the negative and limiting programming that has kept you stuck or feeling broken most of your life.

The problem that most of us have is that we never were taught how to find the real reason we feel the way we do. I see it all over the media and social media that everyone else is to blame. No one wants to be responsible for their "own" thoughts and feelings. They just want to believe that the reason they feel the way they do is because someone else caused it. However, if you want to end the negative results in your life, having the awareness to uncover the thoughts that triggered your emotions will help break the cycle of false programming. This awareness will help you get to the root cause of why you act the way you do and the root thought that is causing your pain and suffering.

Oprah Winfrey, one of the most influential media personalities, often spoke about her journey to self-awareness. Growing up in poverty and experiencing numerous personal challenges, Oprah's self-awareness journey involved recognizing her worth, understanding her emotions, and using her experiences to fuel her success. Her story underscores the importance of awareness of one's past and emotions in shaping a successful and fulfilling life.

"Awareness is the greatest agent for change."
– Eckhart Tolle

Eckhart Tolle, the author of *The Power of Now*, experienced a profound personal crisis in his late twenties, leading to intense anxiety and depression. One night, he had an awakening experience where he realized that his thoughts and emotions were not his true self. This shift in awareness led him to a deep sense of peace and the realization of the present moment's importance.

Awareness is one of the keys to transformation, enabling us to expand from our current situations and experiences. Becoming aware puts the focus on aspects of our lives that need change. Through this heightened awareness, we uncover the areas where growth is needed, allowing us to make conscious choices so we can take deliberate actions toward personal development. Just as my late wife used different lenses to create stunning images, we use awareness to transform our lives, achieving clarity and insight that propel us toward our goals and aspirations.

One of the most powerful things I discovered was a specific journaling practice that gave me deeper insights and revelations about myself. I uncovered the root cause of many emotions that held me hostage for years, and it allowed me to recognize the stories that were limiting my life and keeping me trapped. It created a deeper awareness and understanding in me that the reality, the outer world I see, is just a reflection of the world living inside me.

Action

To start your journey in creating a higher level of awareness, open your journal and ask yourself the following question:

- In what area of your life would you like to practice greater awareness?
- Go to the table you created in the last chapter, and in each category, ask yourself:
- What about this (area) do I need to be more aware of to improve this area of my life?

Additional questions can be found in the book bonuses.

ACCEPTANCE

STOP FIGHTING WHAT IS

> "You can't go back and change the beginning, but you can start where you are and change the ending."
> – **C.S. Lewis**

After my wife passed away in 2011, I was extremely devastated and broken for many months to come. I allowed the belief, "I need to find someone to feel happy again," to be a focal point, and just after a year, I remarried. However, instead of finding happiness, I found more problems than I could handle and was more miserable than ever. The relationship was filled with constant arguments and petty conflicts over my children or her children. When it inevitably ended in divorce, I convinced myself it was just a fluke—I believed I knew how to build a successful relationship, having done so for many years before. So, once again, I pursued another relationship. But as I described in the introduction of this book, that too ended in divorce.

At that point in my life, I decided to step back and embrace where I was, even though the thoughts of being alone would creep in, bringing that familiar ache in my gut. I realized the best thing I could do was to learn how to find happiness in my current situation. If I could find contentment in this station of life, I could rebuild my relationships with my children and rediscover true satisfaction. By focusing on being happy where I was in life, I left the door open to attract the "ONE"—the right someone who would love and accept me for who I truly am.

On my whiteboard, I wrote the words "Attract the One." I was no longer going to chase after people who didn't align with me or feed into co-dependent relationships. Instead, I committed to working on myself and becoming the best version of myself. By doing so, I believed my energy would radiate outward, like a radio antenna broadcasting its signal, and I would naturally attract the right person into my life. Whether or not she showed up, I was determined to be happy and focus on the things I could control.

I started my next level of transformation by waking up to my current reality in all the key areas of my life. I took a hard and honest assessment of where I was with my health and well-being, both spiritually and emotionally, financially, and with my family and friends.

My poor choices during the years preceding this undertaking had heavily affected my relationships. The tremendous loss and suffering, along with the difficult emotions of grief, depression, sorrow, sadness, anger, and regret, wreaked a heavy toll on my body and mind. I felt very much like the wounded dog who wants to crawl into a hole and hide so it can recover. The pain from my suffering kept me hidden from the world.

In a broken mental and emotional state, it is natural to want to hide and not feel like building relationships or working on improving anything in your life. In this state, it becomes easy to fall even deeper into depression and to sedate yourself with the things that might bring you instant pleasure. My go-to strategy was eating lots of ice cream and binge-watching Netflix.

Then, one day, after much study and reflection, I caught myself telling the same story for what seemed like the one-hundredth time. I realized that the reason why we tell the same story repeatedly lies deep inside of us and is due to unprocessed emotions and unresolved issues in our minds. Our current reality doesn't match the paradigm we were taught or learned, or our programming tells us that we shouldn't be experiencing what we are currently experiencing.

This often occurs in the **acceptance** phase of the grief cycle, and I have known many widowed and divorced individuals who have been stuck for years and can't seem to move forward with creating a new life.

It was finally when I told myself, **"The past cannot be changed! No matter what, it cannot and will not change. I must accept where I am today!"** Then the floodgates opened, and the emotions I held so tightly guarded burst from the broken dam in my heart. I could finally let go of what was keeping me stuck. Now, telling the story that was so emotionally charged before now no longer has the same sting or pain associated with it.

Acceptance isn't a one-time deal. It is not a do-it-once-and-you're-done operation. There must be a frequent practice of accepting "what is" and letting go.

Acceptance isn't just about the grief cycle. It is everywhere. It can be put into a daily practice of accepting "what is." "What is" are the facts of life that can't be changed. **They are the circumstances and situations that you try to argue against.**

When someone cuts you off in traffic, road rage ensues because you don't want to accept what just happened, and you want to make the jerk pay for whatever it is.

When someone shows up an hour late after they told you not to be late and they would be there on time.

When your computer's hard drive crashes and you lose two weeks' worth of work because you have no backup.

When your house is only a few years old, and your roof starts to leak.

When you have been performing at a peak level at your job, given an exceptional rating and stock grants to keep you there, then your company turns around and tells you after nearly thirty years of service that your position has been eliminated, and you are asked to leave without even a "thank you." Yet the lower-performing guys you've been carrying on your back still have their job.

These situations can cause you a lot of mental and emotional pain and suffering in your life if you are trying to control or change the outcome. I am sure you have gone through the mental exercise of asking, "Why me? Why did this have to happen to me?" and then making up some outlandish story about what happened. It is also emotionally exhausting and painful to rehearse all the situations and stories you want to change.

In some situations, finding the "why" can lead to you influencing change for the better. But in most cases, you are just arguing against reality. **The real reason you sit and ruminate in situations is that your brain is trying to make what is irrational rational.** If your brain thinks something is out of the norm, it will not make sense, and you will feel uneasy and stressed.

The brain is wired to seek coherence and understanding, especially in emotionally significant or distressing situations. When faced with these situations, the brain engages in repetitive thinking to try to find a solution or a logical explanation, even if this effort ultimately leads to increased stress and negative emotions.

Multiple studies have identified that people who are experiencing depression are more prone to rumination and have repetitive thoughts of shame, anger, regret, and sorrow.

When you can accept "what is," you will find peace.

You can then let go of the negative, unwanted emotions and won't have to create a fictitious story about how the person who didn't respond to you hates you. Or that the person who just cut you off was intentionally trying to kill you.

In my research, I encountered acceptance and commitment therapy (ACT therapy). It is a type of mindful psychotherapy that helps you stay focused on the present moment and accept thoughts and feelings without judgment. It aims to help you move forward through difficult emotions so you can put your energy into healing instead of dwelling on the negative.

Little did I know at the time that I had come up with a method on my own that follows this process. I believe in divine inspiration from God, and I know He will give us what we need when we ask for it. And I love it when I find evidence of the same truth elsewhere. The inspiration came at a moment of great despair, and I want to share it with you:

If you want to change your life, you must love yourself the way you are and surrender to "what is." Forgive yourself and let go! This will allow space to open up to create the future you desire.

I remember the day I hired a life coach. He had me write down a list of affirmations about myself. He then told me to get up from the kitchen table, go to the bathroom just off the side of the kitchen, and look in the mirror. Standing behind me, he directed me to read my affirmations out loud while I looked at myself in the mirror. I began to read them, and he stopped me immediately and said, "Stop! I want you to read them with emphasis and power." So I began again, and as I stood there, delivering these statements with energy and looking into my own eyes in the mirror, the tears started to well up and then pour out of my eyes. I felt the painful emotions buried deep in me begin to rise inside me.

Now a host of negative emotions were pouring out of me. I felt anger, frustration, regret, guilt, shame, loneliness, despair, and hopelessness. What a relief it was to let out these pent-up emotions finally. That day, I recognized that I didn't love myself and needed to do something about it.

This event opened opportunities for me to learn meditation and start a daily meditation practice that has changed my life. I devised a daily meditation that I would start my day off with that helped me **accept** life for what it is and let go of pent-up emotions by forgiving myself.

> *"The curious paradox is that when I accept myself just as I am, then I can change."*
> **– Carl Rogers**

Loving yourself becomes quite challenging in a world overflowing with comparison and criticism. Loving yourself as you are—including your good and bad choices, mistakes, regrets, appearance, manner of speaking, and everything else—is essential for growth and transformation.

Action

Open your journal and answer the following questions:

- Where do you feel the most anger, regret, guilt, or shame about (Health & Fitness, Wellness, Relationships, Income, etc.)?
- What is the one thought that comes up the most about this?
- What feelings come up for you about this?
- By accepting these experiences in your life, what lessons can you learn from the experience?
- How does knowing these lessons make you feel?

OWNERSHIP

TAKE RESPONSIBILITY

> *"You must take personal responsibility. You cannot change the circumstances, the seasons, or the wind, but you can change yourself."*
> **– Jim Rohn**

On your journey to becoming the creator of the life of your dreams, you can no longer operate from the mindset **"life happens to me,"** blaming everyone around you for your current life circumstances. You will need to operate from a new mindset, **"life happens for me,"** giving up the blame and taking 100 percent responsibility for your thoughts and emotions.

After Amy's death, the question of **"WHY?"** would trouble me daily.

Why did this have to happen to me and my family?

Haven't I gone through enough already?
God, are you really there?

I believe in God and that he still provides miracles to his children on Earth, but what happened to me left a huge hole in my heart and many questions that I wanted answers to. Highly emotional experiences can change your life because it is easy to allow incoming negative thoughts to undermine programming that formerly brought about good results. They might also cause you to introduce beliefs about things contradictory to your original belief system.

In that situation, it would have been easy for me to conclude that God doesn't exist, that He doesn't love me, or that I must have done something wrong and was being punished. These thoughts could have easily formed a new belief, especially since the painful experiences I was going through might seem to support it. My brain would then quickly start collecting more evidence to reinforce this belief, and before long, I would have created a mental program running on autopilot. Each time something went wrong, it would only further validate the idea that God either doesn't exist or doesn't care.

The alternative to believing thoughts that pass through our minds randomly and are trying to take root is to **question them and not instantly assume they're true**.

Taking full responsibility for your results means recognizing that you are the creator of your outcomes.

As the creator of your life, you must regularly pause in different situations and ask yourself:

"Will this thought create what I want in this situation?"

And I have often changed the course of a disagreement by asking myself:

"What must I think or do to create what I want in this situation?"

In each instance, a thought will arise that results in a better outcome than you are used to experiencing.

If you want to be the creator of your life, you must not play victim to every thought or emotion that passes through you. You can and should question them.

If I let the thought stick around that "God doesn't love me and just wants to punish me," it would bring about a lot of negative emotions, and over time, the actions it would produce in life would be the same as lighting a torch and setting my home on fire.

Asking myself, **"What must I think to create what I want?"** I was told to use prayer to seek the truth. Over time, God gave me the answers I sought. One of the many answers was that **God does love us.**

Owning Your Feelings

Have you ever been blamed for hurting someone's feelings? What if your intent was good? You might even be thinking, "What just happened here?" This kind of thing happens way too often in relationships.

Take Responsibility

You must start owning your emotions. They originate from within you.

Our thoughts shape how we feel. Someone might smile at you, and you think, "They like me," leading to a feeling of happiness. On the other hand, if you had the thought, "They are laughing at me," it might lead to a feeling of embarrassment.

Suppose you're going to speak in front of a large crowd. You may think, "I am not good enough," and you would feel very anxious. Or if you think, "This is an amazing opportunity," you might feel excited.

Your thoughts, positive or negative, will lead to positive or negative emotions. What you tell yourself on a day-to-day basis does matter and will affect how you feel.

The book *Switch on Your Brain* by Dr. Caroline Leaf provides a detailed explanation of the scientific mechanisms by which thoughts influence emotions. And how different thoughts trigger specific neurochemical reactions that result in various emotional states.

The next time you get triggered emotionally, I want you to ask yourself, **"What story am I telling myself?"** that has caused me to feel this way. And ask, **"What meaning am I giving this story that I am telling myself?"**

When you start to understand that it isn't other people who are making you feel a certain way, you begin to take back control of your life. You have more power than you think to control how you feel in life. Owning what you feel in the moment is powerful. Tony Robbins is always talking about your state and controlling how you think and feel. I recall one interview he had where he described how hard he had worked to create the person he had become.

Live in the state you want. This doesn't mean stuffing down negative emotions and not feeling them; it means starting to create what you want by being aware of what you think and tell yourself daily.

Owning Your Actions

Being a creator of your life means choosing to take action in the areas that you want to develop and grow. **Life will throw all kinds of challenges at you. And there are only two things that you can control: your thoughts about the situation and your response to it.**

You get to choose how to act when anything happens to you. If you get laid off from your job, you can choose to sit and cry about it and feel depressed for weeks on end about how unfair it was, or you can choose to get up and do something about it.

My father opened his gym, Alpha Health Spa, when I was a young boy. It was just a simple gym that men attended on Tuesday, Thursday, and Saturday and women on Monday, Wednesday, and Friday. It later grew into the Alpha Fitness Center, which has all the spa and recreational center amenities.

Take Responsibility

At eight years old, I remember him flipping on the light switch early every morning before school. He would say, "Rise and shine!" It was time to go to work. The whole family worked in the business. My siblings and I were janitors, and I remember vacuuming, emptying the garbage, and cleaning bathrooms for most of my childhood. We would clean the spa before we went to school every day and before opening on Saturday. Over the years, my father trained us to do various aspects of the business, including being fitness instructors, sales reps, and even managers.

He expanded the business and relocated the family to the Midwest, where we opened several more fitness centers. When I was around twenty, he sold the company to some of his employees, but within a few years, he had to regain control. Around that time, a new fitness trend was emerging, driven by Nautilus equipment, and a competitor called 24 Hour Nautilus opened in town. It was co-ed and operated 24/7.

In response, we updated our gyms to be co-ed and equipped with the latest weightlifting machines. We also converted a few locations to operate twenty-four hours a day to stay competitive. The new competitor flooded the market with cheap memberships, overcrowding their gyms. However, after about a year, they went out of business. We made it easy for their members to transition to our gyms, but this left all our locations packed.

Just as we were adjusting, another company came in, took over the failed competitor's buildings, and repeated the cycle of selling discounted memberships. They, too, eventually went under. My father decided to take over some of their locations to eliminate competition, but by then, he had exhausted his savings and remortgaged the house. By the time I was twenty-five, married with two children, my father was forced to sell the business at a loss. He lost everything—the business, home, cars, truck, boat, and motorhome. On top of that, he faced a significant tax debt that had to be paid.

At fifty-three, my dad, mom, and two sisters moved to Utah to start fresh. He rented a place and began a new career in the insurance industry. Over time, he paid off his tax debt, bought a house, and eventually paid that off. Life had dealt him some very tough challenges beyond his control, and though he fought through them the best way he knew how, what I admire most about him is that I never once heard him complain. He didn't dwell on his past failures and struggles or blame others. Instead, he got up each day and worked hard; when the time came, he played hard, too.

I admired my father's example of accepting what was no longer in his control and taking responsibility for his life. Taking the right action is always the best remedy for creating your desired outcome. If we sit and let our emotions overwhelm us with negativity, then the actions that follow will most certainly be negative. However, if you want positive results in life, there must be positive actions preceded by positive emotions and thoughts.

When you take responsibility for your life, you can stop living by the victim mindset of **"life happens to me."** You can start to see the lessons that life is gifting you so that you can become the creator of it. A creator's mind is that life is full of lessons and that **"life happens for me."**

Taking full responsibility for your life starts by:

- Knowing you are 100 percent responsible for your own thoughts and feelings
- Finding the lesson
- Creating a new outcome

Creating a new outcome starts by:

- Thinking things will work out
- Believing and feeling they will
- Waiting and watching new doors open
- Taking action and walking through

Action

Let's open your journal and answer the following prompts about taking responsibility.

- Where in your life do you need to take 100 percent responsibility?
- What victim stories are you telling yourself about this?
- How does it make you feel when you tell yourself these stories?
- What actions do you take or fail to take when you tell yourself these stories?

THE FRAME

DEFINING THE "LENS" OF REALITY

> *"When you change the way you look at things, the things you look at change."*
> **– Wayne Dyer**

I vividly remember sitting in physics class, learning about frames of reference. The concept was simple but fascinating—a frame of reference is like a set of coordinates used to measure where things are and how they move. The best example? Sitting on a moving train. Everything inside the train felt still to me, but to someone outside, I was moving right along with it.

The same applies to how we see life. In the social sciences, a frame of reference refers to the assumptions and beliefs we use to make sense of the world. Our mental and emotional filters are shaped by our personal experiences, values, and attitudes.

That image of sitting on the train has always stuck with me because it's a powerful metaphor for how our perspectives shape our reality. Like switching from the view inside the train to outside, changing our mental frame of reference can dramatically shift how we perceive life's events, people, and challenges. When we learn to recognize and adjust these frames, we gain a clearer, more balanced view, turning obstacles into opportunities. If we want to live a purpose-driven life, we need to get good at changing our frame of reference.

Our personal frame of reference doesn't pop up randomly; it's built over time through our experiences, beliefs, and the environment we grew up in. Everything from our upbringing to our relationships plays a role in shaping the way we see the world.

One of my favorite examples of this comes from the movie *The Matrix*. In a scene, Neo asks a boy how he can bend a spoon. The boy replies, "Don't try to bend the spoon. That's impossible. Instead, realize the truth…there is no spoon." He explains that it's not the spoon bending but Neo's perception that changes. This idea is spot-on when it comes to frames of reference. We often see limitations and barriers, which are usually shaped by our minds. Our challenges, like the spoon, are not the things that need to change—we are.

Think about it: how many of our relationships, or our struggles, could completely transform if we simply shifted how we viewed them?

For example, take two people I know who lost their spouses but with stark contrasts and views of life.

Person 1: "I'm done. I've tried everything. Nothing works, and I don't want to keep trying."

Person 2: "Life is beautiful! Even at seventy-six, I'm still setting goals, climbing new mountains, and loving every moment."

Two people had the same life event, but their frame of reference made all the difference in how they responded.

So where do you see yourself?

Elements of the Frame

If we want to understand and reshape how we see things, we must break down the components that make up our frame of reference. Think of it like a computer program running in the background of your life. The four key elements are **rules, beliefs, experiences**, and **environment**.

These define the filter we use to gather information about our reality. Sometimes they help us, but often, they hold us back. Outdated **rules** tell us what we should or shouldn't do, limiting our creativity. **Beliefs**, especially negative ones, can sabotage our confidence. Past **experiences**, particularly tough ones, reinforce those negative beliefs, keeping us stuck. And our **environment**? That's what shapes our daily habits, attitudes, and actions. If it's toxic or unsupportive, it'll keep you from growing.

Together, these elements form the lens through which we see the world. If your lens is fogged up with old rules, limiting beliefs, and negative experiences, you will see the world in a distorted way. But here's the exciting part: you can change the lens.

Reprogramming your frame of reference means reexamining the rules you live by, questioning whether they still serve you, and updating them to align with your true values. It means reshaping your beliefs to empower you instead of holding you back. It also involves reframing past experiences, seeing them as lessons rather than setbacks. And it requires cultivating an environment that supports your growth.

By doing this, you clear and expand your lens, allowing you to see yourself and the world in a new, more empowering light. The result? A life that reflects your true potential, filled with purpose and meaning.

Action

Let's take a minute to understand your frame:

- What area in your life requires the most work (health/fitness, mental/spiritual, relationships, career/business, etc.)?
- What are some rules that you have in that area?
- What are some of your beliefs about this?
- What experiences have you had that have led you to this point in your life?
- What does your current environment look like? Supportive or unsupportive?

THE REFRAME
SEEING LIFE WITH NEW EYES

> *"The real voyage of discovery consists not in seeking new landscapes, but in having new eyes."*
> **— Marcel Proust**

Reframing is one of the most powerful tools for completely transforming and elevating your life. Everything you've learned so far has led you to this game-changing concept. It's about shifting the lens through which you see your current reality. When you change your perception, you break free from the limiting patterns that have kept you stuck, unlocking a new world full of opportunities and potential.

Why You Must Learn to Reframe

Understanding how to reframe is essential because it allows you to shift from a limited, negative perspective to a more expansive, positive one. **This shift is not just about feeling better; it is about how to become the creator of your life.** Reframing helps you to see opportunities where you once saw obstacles, to find lessons in failures, and to transform stress into excitement. These changes in perception will lead to more proactive behaviors and better results in every aspect of your life, and you will become the creator you were meant to be.

Understanding Reframing

Reframing is changing the context or meaning of a situation to view it from a different perspective. **It's like putting on a new pair of glasses that transform how you see the world.** When you reframe a situation, you **shift your focus** from what's wrong to right, from problems to possibilities. Remember the Reticular Activating System (RAS) in your brain, which responds to what you focus on and filters your experiences accordingly. By reframing, you create a new reality by directing your RAS to highlight positive aspects and opportunities instead of obstacles.

Consider the story of Dr. Viktor Frankl, a Holocaust survivor and renowned psychiatrist, who wrote about his experiences in the concentration camps in his book *Man's Search for Meaning*. Frankl reframed his suffering by finding meaning in it. **He believed that**

even in the most horrific conditions, individuals could choose their attitude and find purpose. This reframing helped him survive the camps and later develop his theory of logotherapy, which has helped countless people find meaning in their lives. Frankl's ability to reframe his circumstances shows how powerful this technique can be in transforming one's reality.

Reframing Failure to Success

Imagine you've just failed an important exam. The immediate reaction might be disappointment and self-criticism. However, if you were to ask yourself, **"What can I learn from this experience? How can I improve?"** You could turn this into a learning opportunity and shift your perspective, transforming failures into stepping stones for future success.

Michael Jordan, widely regarded as one of the greatest basketball players of all time, is famous for his successes and perspective on failure. He once said, "I've missed more than 9,000 shots in my career. I've lost almost 300 games. Twenty-six times, I've been trusted to take the game-winning shot and missed. I've failed over and over and over again in my life. And that is why I succeed." Jordan reframed his **failures as essential steps toward his success**, allowing him to maintain the confidence and drive needed to become a legend in his sport.

Michael changed how he viewed failure. This has been one of my greatest hurdles, preventing me from trying new things in life because of my perfectionist mindset. It's been a struggle to push myself out of my comfort zone and allow myself to fail so that I can succeed. I love this next story of how one father's reframe led to his daughter's success.

Sara Blakely, the founder of Spanx, grew up with a father who had an unconventional approach to failure. Each night at dinner, he would ask Sara and her brother, **"What did you fail at today?"** Celebrating their failures, he redefined what failure meant. Instead of seeing failure as a negative outcome, Sara learned it was about taking action and trying and learned to see it as an essential part of growth and learning. This reframing of failure as a positive experience allowed her to take risks and persist through challenges, ultimately leading to her success as a billionaire entrepreneur.

Reframing Setbacks to Opportunities

Imagine you have been excelling at your job, playing a crucial role in your project's success. During your previous yearly review, you were rated exceptional and awarded stock grants to ensure you stayed with the company. Anticipating the upcoming year-end review, you looked forward to discussing promotions and raises due to your stellar performance.

To your surprise, you are called into a meeting with the director, who says, "I am sorry. We have to let you go today. Your position has been eliminated." The shock and horror of the news can be overwhelming. You could easily become bitter and resentful, spending weeks ruminating on how this could happen to you.

However, you could also reframe this setback as a new opportunity handed to you. This unexpected change can be seen as a chance to pursue all the things you've been wanting to do but never had the time or courage for.

That was my story, and it caught me by great surprise. Instead of dwelling on the negative, I chose to see it as an opportunity for growth and new beginnings. This mindset shift made all the difference in how I moved forward.

Thomas Edison, one of the greatest inventors in history, experienced a devastating fire at his laboratory in 1914. The fire destroyed years of work and caused millions of dollars in damage. Instead of seeing this as a catastrophe, Edison reframed the situation. He reportedly told his son, "Thank goodness all our mistakes were burned up. Now we can start fresh again." This reframing allowed Edison to move forward with renewed energy and creativity, ultimately leading to more successful inventions.

Journey to Success

J.K. Rowling, now one of the world's most successful authors, faced numerous challenges before achieving her fame. In the early 1990s, she was a single mother living on welfare, struggling to support her daughter, Jessica, after her marriage had failed. Battling clinical depression, Rowling found solace in writing, developing the story of a young wizard named Harry Potter.

Despite her dire financial situation, she continued to write, often in cafes while her daughter slept beside her. When she finished the manuscript for *Harry Potter and the Philosopher's Stone*, Rowling faced numerous rejections from publishers. **Twelve different publishers turned her down, doubting the marketability of a children's book about a young wizard.** However, **Rowling believed in her story and persisted**.

Finally, Bloomsbury, a small London publisher, agreed to publish her book. Even then, the initial print run was modest, and Rowling was advised to get a day job. Despite these doubts, the book quickly gained popularity, and Rowling's life began to change. The success of *Harry Potter and the Philosopher's Stone* was just the beginning. The book won several awards and captivated readers worldwide. Rowling wrote six more books in the series, each more successful than the last.

Rowling's journey is a powerful example of reframing setbacks into opportunities. Instead of succumbing to despair, she saw her difficult circumstances as temporary and used them as motivation to pursue her passion for writing. Her story illustrates the incredible impact of perseverance and the power of believing in oneself. By reframing her struggles as opportunities for growth and creativity, J.K. Rowling transformed her life and achieved extraordinary success, inspiring countless others to see setbacks as stepping stones to their dreams.

The Birth of a New Reality

When you start seeing life through a different set of lenses, you are expanding your consciousness to open up to infinite possibilities. When your perspective changes, so does your focus, and it profoundly impacts your thoughts, feelings, and actions. When you change the way you view a situation, you also change how you think about it, how you feel about it, and how you respond to it. This shift leads to more positive outcomes and a more empowered approach to life. You are now becoming the creator of your new reality.

Think of your personal growth and transformation like a set of Russian dolls. Each time you change your perspective, you grow into a bigger and better version of yourself. Like how each Russian doll fits into a larger one, every new perspective builds on the last, making you more expansive and enriched. This ongoing process of shifting your view and growing helps you unlock new layers of potential, turning you into a more empowered and fulfilled person. Say goodbye to the old and welcome the new whenever you change your perspective.

The shift to a new perspective profoundly impacts your thoughts, feelings, and actions. When you change how you view a situation, you also change how you think about it, how you feel about it, and how you respond to it. This shift creates a new version of you with more positive outcomes and a more empowered approach to life.

Your new lens of reality impacts your thoughts because they can't stay the same in this new reality as they once were in the old one. By creating new thoughts, you will, in turn, create new feelings and emotions. You will feel more optimistic and less stressed. And when your thoughts and feelings are aligned positively, your actions follow suit. You will develop more proactive and constructive behaviors that produce better results. This will become a perpetual cycle of reframing and recreating yourself hour by hour, day by day, and month by month. After a short time, you will not recognize the person that you have become.

Action

Take a few minutes to journal on the following questions:

- From the previous chapter, what is the one thing you would like to change the most?
- Why do you want change to occur in this area?
- When you think about the "why", what emotions arise about this?
- When you feel this emotion, what thoughts come up?
- What are you telling yourself about this situation to keep feeling this way?

A full process for discovering your frame is at e3blueprint.com/bookbonus.

REWRITING YOUR STORIES

> "I am writing my story and I alone have the responsibility to shape it into something meaningful."
> **– Charlotte Eriksson**
>
> "It becomes obvious that if we want to make relatively minor changes in our lives, we can perhaps appropriately focus on our attitudes and behaviors. But if we want to make significant, quantum change, we need to work on our basic paradigms."
> **– Dr. Stephen Covey**

Learning to change and rewrite your stories is one of the most important pivotal steps in creating a new reality. The next significant push is expanding your consciousness and learning how to tap into its full potential. This journey enables you to raise your vibrational frequency, attracting and manifesting abundance. It empowers you to be the true creator of your destiny. God wants us to learn to be like Him, and these lessons are fundamental steps in that evolution. God has granted us agency, the right to choose how we live this life, making us the authors of our own stories. It is up to us to write our narratives and take responsibility for shaping them into something meaningful.

Some might argue that God is writing our stories, and we have no control. While God does guide and direct us, He also grants us the autonomy to grow on our own. In my own life, I can show you two stark examples. A dear friend of mine, who was suffering from hardships in his relationship, chose to take his own life, drastically affecting his friends and family. On the other hand, I know of others, myself included, who have faced tragic and difficult experiences but have chosen to reframe and grow. Through this choice, we have found happiness and fulfillment.

In his book, *As a Man Thinketh*, James Allen states: "**Man is buffeted by circumstances so long as he believes himself to be the creature of outside conditions**, but when he realizes that **he is a creative power** and that he may command the hidden soil and seeds of his being out of which circumstances grow, he then becomes the rightful master of himself."

Your thoughts have immense power. Whether you believe that God grants you the power to create your destiny or not, your reality will be shaped by that belief.

Your thoughts are the seeds from which your circumstances grow, and recognizing this power can transform your life.

You are the creator of your story. However, it's up to you to decide if you want to include God in its creation. Believing that He exists and allowing Him to assist you in your efforts will bring about miraculous results in your life.

The Stories Are the Programming

The stories we tell ourselves are the mental scripts that shape our internal programming. This programming consists of our rules, beliefs, attitudes, and expectations, which influence our frames and behaviors. These internal stories build the frame and create the lens on how we interpret our experiences and the world around us, acting as a filter through which all information is processed.

This internal programming begins developing from the moment we are born. Our early experiences, interactions with caregivers, and the messages we receive from our environment all contribute to the formation of our core beliefs and attitudes. As children, from zero to seven, we absorb information like sponges directly into our subconscious mind.

The conscious mind's critical thinking and filtering processes are not fully developed, allowing experiences, beliefs, and information to be embedded deeply into the subconscious mind. Our brains then create neural pathways that solidify our understanding of the world. These pathways are reinforced by repeated experiences and the stories we construct to make sense of them.

For example, if a child consistently receives positive reinforcement and encouragement, they are likely to develop a strong sense of self-worth and capability. Conversely, if a child frequently encounters criticism or neglect, they may internalize beliefs of inadequacy and unworthiness. These early narratives become the foundation of our internal programming, influencing our thoughts, feelings, and actions throughout life.

This is the programming that most of us have to deal with on a day-to-day basis, telling us how to live our lives. So, if you are fifty years old, you still have an eight-year-old in your head telling you how life is supposed to be lived unless you start rewriting and rewiring that old programming.

If you are consistently telling yourself a particular story, whether it is empowering or limiting, it becomes ingrained in your subconscious mind. For example, if you tell yourself the story that you are not good enough, this belief becomes part of your programming, affecting your confidence and actions. On the other hand, if you tell yourself the story that you are capable and resilient, this positive belief shapes your programming, encouraging proactive and constructive behavior.

The difference is that as an adult, you have a fully developed prefrontal cortex that can act as a filter and interpreter of information that enters the mind, allowing you to determine whether to believe or question the validity of a story.

We can reprogram and rewire our minds by finding the old stories and rewriting them. Rewriting our narratives is a reframing process, and it will cause the old faulty programming to stop where new, improved programming can be installed. If a more positive, empowering belief can be installed, it can transform our internal programming, giving us a new, improved lens and creating a reality that is much more fulfilling and successful.

> "We don't see things as they are, we see them as we are. The stories we tell ourselves create our reality."
> **– Anaïs Nin**

Search and Destroy

Our biggest problem is that the majority of our programming, which runs our daily life, runs silently.

Do you even know why you do half the things you do?
Why haven't you achieved your greatest desires and dreams?
What keeps you stuck in a hamster wheel of thoughts?
What is causing your procrastination toward your latest goals?

Why do you fear doing things that you don't have certainty about?

These answers and more can be found deep in your subconscious mind. Over the years, I have hired therapists, hypnotherapists, and coaches and spent thousands on programs to weed the garden of my mind. Over time I discovered and created a way to go on a search and destroy mission of my own to find the faulty and negative programming and to rewrite it so that I could then start to manifest happiness and joy in my life. You, too, can go on your own mission to search and destroy the negative old programming that has limited your life and stopped you from creating the life you want.

When you take on the responsibility of finding and rewriting your programming, you'll be amazed at the ripple effect you will create in your life and how every change you make can change your life.

With every program rewritten and new rule, belief, or perspective implemented comes a new reality and a new version of yourself.

Action

The first step in rewriting your stories is to identify them. If you are already emotionally charged about something, or the next time you find yourself emotionally triggered, pull out your journal, and let's do some work.

- What emotion am I experiencing at this moment?
- What is the situation that created this feeling I am experiencing?
- Who or what is involved in triggering me to feel this way?
- What am I telling myself about this situation? What story am I telling? (This can take some time; allow your subconscious a few minutes to uncover what you are telling yourself.)

Once the old faulty story has been uncovered, you can begin work on rewriting a new empowering story. Go to e3blueprint.com/bookbonus for detailed instructions on how to rewrite these old stories.

TRANSFORMATION

EMBRACING THE PATH TO EXPAND

> *"The greatest discovery of my generation is that a human being can alter his life by altering his attitudes."*
> **– William James**

Let's wrap up this topic of expansion. It is critically important to remember why this topic is so important. When your current reality is defined by the elements of your rules, beliefs, experiences, and environment, it forms this nice little box called reality that you create for yourself, which I compared to *The Matrix*. This box confines you and limits you to living within its parameters.

Most people will coast through life living within the confines of their current reality; however, a small percentage of people like yourself are looking to live a bigger life. This requires you to break from the confines of your current parameters and expand beyond the borders of the box you have created for yourself.

Once you have broken free from the old reality you were living in and created a new reality, you will find you are now living inside a new box with a new set of elements that you have defined at this next level. The process begins over again, expanding yourself and breaking free to a newer and greater you.

In each new box that you find yourself in, you will follow a similar path of waking up to the reality that you are in and finding the lies you are telling yourself about this new reality. Then, by using your newly developed habit of being aware, you can start identifying the patterns and limiting beliefs that are defining the confines of this new reality, laying the groundwork for the inner transformation that must occur to break free to the next level.

This all might sound hard, but like starting any new habit with persistence, it gets easier and easier over time. Just as our muscles grow stronger through regular exercise, our consciousness and personal development expand through consistent effort and reflection. If we stop challenging ourselves and stop nurturing our growth, we risk a kind of atrophy—not just of the body, but of the mind and spirit. With continued practice, you will identify the sticking points to your new future rather quickly.

With each new version of your reality, you will have to "stop fighting what is" and come to terms with the elements keeping you stuck by releasing your resistance to your newfound confines and the unnecessary suffering it brings. Acceptance and letting go open the door to many new possibilities, allowing you to expand to the newer version of yourself. Accepting "what is" before you will make it so much easier to move into owning and taking 100 percent responsibility for the direction and velocity your life is going. Taking responsibility gives you the power and control to shape your experiences through conscious choices.

By understanding how your reality is constructed like a box, through your lens of reality and reframing your perspective, you can tear down the walls of limiting beliefs, transforming them into empowering ones. This process of framing and reframing will allow you to view life with fresh eyes and discover new opportunities where you once only saw obstacles.

Finally, you will define the "new you" that will no longer be confined to the past and is ready to step into the future. Each time you want to create a new reality for yourself, you will face the exciting prospect of creating a new identity that aligns with your highest potential. You have the opportunity to write and rewrite the story of your life that embodies your newfound insights and aspirations. Each time you write, it is just a draft that can be rewritten into a better version of the last.

In Search of The Creation Formula

The pursuit of expansion is not a one-time event but a lifelong commitment. Like maintaining physical fitness, nurturing your growth requires ongoing dedication and effort. When you stop seeking expansion, your growth stagnates, and you risk falling back into old patterns and limiting beliefs. Continuous expansion keeps your mind sharp, your heart open, and your spirit vibrant.

As you move forward, remember that this journey of self-discovery and personal growth is ongoing. Each step you take toward expansion strengthens your capacity to create a fulfilling and meaningful life. By embracing the desire to expand, you will continue to evolve, adapt, and thrive in an ever-changing world. Commit yourself to the practice of expansion, knowing that through this continuous process, you realize your fullest potential and craft the life you truly desire.

PHASE 2
ELEVATE

> *"Our outer world will always be a reflection of our inner world. Our level of success is always going to be parallel to our level of personal development. Until we dedicate time each day to developing the person we need to be to create the life we want, success is always going to be a struggle to attain."*
> **– Hal Elrod**

Elevate, the next phase of The Creation Formula, is essential to helping you create new realities for yourself. I say realities because as you progress over time, you are creating new versions of yourself daily. This phase focuses on elevating yourself to a higher state of being and transforming your inner world, which radiates outward and influences every area of your life—your health, relationships, finances, and overall well-being.

In *Breaking the Habit of Being Yourself*, Dr. Joe Dispenza highlights a profound shift in how we understand reality. In the 1700s, Newtonian physics led people to believe that life operated solely on mechanical principles, leaving us with little control over our outcomes. The idea that reality was fixed and predetermined was the norm. However, Dispenza reveals that energy is far more than just a force acting on matter—it's the foundation of all material things, and, most importantly, it responds to the mind.

> *"Energy is the very fabric of all things material, and is responsive to mind."*
> **– Dr. Joe Dispenza**

It wasn't until Einstein's famous equation $E = mC2$ that we could understand that energy and matter were related, and his work showed they were interchangeable. Because of his theories, scientists set out to discover the interesting behavior of light; it could sometimes be observed as a wave (energy) or as a particle (matter). This completely broke the model of the old Newtonian physics, and from all these experiments, quantum physics was born.

The eye-opening thing we learn from quantum physics is that the old way of thinking about the atom was completely wrong and that the quantum model reveals that it is made up mostly of energy: 99.99999 percent energy and .00001 percent matter. So why is that important? Because everything physical in your life is not made of solid matter but made of energy fields and frequency patterns of information.

The other intriguing discovery in quantum physics was the "observer effect," which suggests that the act of observing a phenomenon can alter its outcome. It was found that the observer of tiny particles that make up atoms affected the behavior of energy and matter. Scientists found that electrons exist on an infinite array of possibilities in an invisible field of energy. And, in the moment the observer looks for an electron of an atom, there is a specific point in time and space when all probabilities of the electron collapse into a physical event.

Why is this so impactful?

Imagine a future event in your life based on one of your desires. According to quantum physics, that "reality" already exists as a possibility in the quantum field, simply waiting for you to observe it. Theoretically, if your mind can influence the behavior of electrons, then it could also influence the appearance of any possibility you can envision.

How might your life transform if you could use focused, mindful attention to turn infinite potential outcomes into the "reality" you desire?

Everything physical in your life was first conceived in the mind before it came into existence in the physical world. Your car, your home, your clothes—all were mentally envisioned in someone's mind before they were manifested.

Thoughts and Feeling: Broadcasting Your Signal

How can your desired future be a manifestation of your thoughts and feelings?

Research is ongoing to study how our thoughts and feelings can affect various outcomes in our lives. One such organization is The HeartMath Institute (HMI), established in 1991 by Doc Childre. The institute's work is grounded in "heart coherence," a state in which the heart, mind, and emotions are in energetic alignment and cooperation.

It is well established that thoughts and feelings do produce an electromagnetic field and are energetic in nature. This electrical activity generated in the brain can be measured using Electroencephalography (EEG). Researchers have found that the brain's electrical activity generates electromagnetic waves that can be detected outside the skull.

The HeartMath Institute has studied the concept of heart-brain coherence, which occurs when the electromagnetic waves produced by the brain and heart are in synch. Their research indicates that emotional states can influence the body's electromagnetic field. Specifically, positive emotions tend to create a more coherent heart rhythm, resulting in a more harmonious electromagnetic field around the body. This coherence can be measured using instruments like electrocardiograms (ECGs) and magnetometers, which detect these electromagnetic changes.

In the article "The Energetic Heart," researchers at The HeartMath Institute show that the energetic field generated by the heart permeates every cell of the body and acts like a synchronizing signal to the body, like radio waves. In the electromagnetic signal of the heart, the electrical component of the wave was measured to be sixty times greater than the electrical signal of the brain, and the magnetic signal was measured to be 100 times greater than the brain, and it could be measured several feet away from the body. The study also showed how emotions distinctly alter cardiac rhythmic activity. These changes in electromagnetic, sound pressure and blood pressure waves are produced and "felt" by every cell in the body.

> "The quantum field responds not to what we want, it responds to who we are being."
> **– Dr. Joe Dispenza**

What I hope you are getting from this information is that **you are an antenna broadcasting electromagnetic waves from your heart and mind**. The more elevated your thoughts and emotions are and the more in sync the heart and mind are, the greater the electromagnetic energy you will produce.

Visualize Your Aura

Please take a moment and visualize with me a field of energy that your body is generating. See it as a golden glow of energy extending from your core outward and surrounding your entire body, acting as a force field or shield. This field of energy is pulsating waves of energy like a radio signal broadcasting out to the universe. Now, think of something you are truly grateful for, and let that emotional energy add to your golden radiant glow. You are now broadcasting warm, positive energy.

Your Outer World is a Reflection of Your Inner World

Have you ever been in a group setting when someone you've never met walks into the room, and you can instantly sense a change in the atmosphere? Could you feel their excitement, sadness, or frustration just from their presence?

And then, with just one look, your instinct is confirmed. Not only did you sense their energy, but you can also see it reflected in their posture, facial expressions, and overall presence. Their physical state mirrors the feeling you picked up on.

How can one person walk into a room and instantly light it up, becoming the life of the party, while another can enter and seem to drain the energy from everyone around them?

What you think and feel creates the life around you. You are broadcasting an electrical and magnetic signal out to the quantum field. Your thoughts are the radio broadcast, and your feelings are the magnet that attracts like-minded experiences into your life. This concept is not a new one. In *Think and Grow Rich*, Napoleon Hill emphasizes the powerful influence of thoughts and emotions on one's outcomes. He asserts that when mixed with emotions, thoughts can transform into their physical equivalents.

One of the very first courses I ever took was from Tony Robbins. He emphasizes the importance of "state" in creating change. He believes that our mental and emotional state significantly influences our perceptions and experiences, and to make meaningful changes in life, one must first change one's state.

Your thoughts and emotions have a direct correlation to your life outcomes. What you are "thinking and feeling" habitually or unconsciously affects whether you stay in the confines of your current reality or break free to something greater.

Let's say you keep dwelling on a painful experience from your past—something that caused deep suffering. We've all been there, right? I doubt there's a single person on this planet who hasn't experienced some form of hardship. But if I stay stuck in that mindset, playing the victim to my suffering, I'm constantly sending signals to the quantum field through my thoughts, reinforcing that pain. At the same time, I'm attracting more suffering through the negative emotions I'm generating. It's no surprise then that similar painful experiences keep showing up in my life—it's a cycle I'm unknowingly feeding.

Your State of Being Becomes Your Identity

Let's take a moment to break down what actually creates your state of "being." There's a constant loop between your mind and body, a cycle of thinking and feeling. When you have a thought, your brain triggers a chemical reaction that generates feelings and emotions tied to that thought. Then, because your brain is tuned in to what your body is feeling, it starts to think in alignment with those emotions. This creates more chemicals, leading to more feelings, and the cycle repeats. You end up feeling the way you think and thinking the way you feel, locking yourself in a loop.

The state where the mind and body are in unison is a "state of being." **Who you are "being" is what you are consistently thinking and feeling.** When someone uses the words "*I am happy*," "*I am angry*," or "*I am depressed*," they are describing a state of being. Because thoughts cause chemical reactions in the mind, causing feelings and emotions in the body. They get stored in the body as a memory, and when you replay that loop or memory enough times, it becomes your identity.

I remember hitting my thirties and struggling with depression. Back then, people would just say, "It's all in your thoughts—what you're thinking is causing your depression." But now I understand that when this loop of thoughts and feelings repeats over and over, it gets memorized and stored in the body like a program. I'd wake up in the morning, and without even having a single thought, my body automatically shifted into that familiar feeling of depression. I used to try to analyze my thoughts, asking myself, "What am I thinking that's making me feel this way?"—but I couldn't pinpoint anything. Yet, because I felt depressed, the thoughts would eventually start creeping in to match the feeling, and I'd get stuck in the cycle of feeling down and thinking thoughts that reinforced it.

It becomes ingrained in your identity when you remain stuck in a particular state of being for an extended period. You start labeling yourself with statements like, "I am a depressed person," "I am an introvert," "I am anxious," "I'm not good enough," or "I'm not that smart." Over time, this state of being turns into a habit, becoming part of your personality. The challenge with breaking this habit is that it's no longer just about changing your thoughts—your body has memorized this state, and it's now running on autopilot at a subconscious level.

How do you get unstuck and out of the negative thought and feeling loop?

To get unstuck, you must start thinking beyond your current feelings. Albert Einstein once said, "No problem can be solved from the same level of consciousness that created it." If you want to elevate yourself, you need to shift your thinking. When you begin thinking greater than your feelings, your mind will generate emotions that align with those elevated thoughts, creating an upward spiral that moves you forward.

In addition, you'll need to actively generate and practice positive emotions that go beyond your current thoughts. When you begin practicing feeling better than your usual thinking, your mind will respond by producing thoughts that align with those elevated emotions.

Since your old habits of thinking and feeling kept you stuck, creating a new habit is key. With time and repetition, this new habit will override the old one, rewiring your brain with an empowering mindset that moves you forward.

Thinking + Feeling + Action = Results

Let's take the concepts you're reading one step further and add actions to the equation. When you have a thought there is a chemical reaction that causes you to have an associated feeling and emotion. What follows the feelings is an action or reaction to the emotion you experienced. **Your actions are what create the results in your life.**

For example, if you're about to give a speech in front of a large audience and you think, "I'm going to embarrass myself during this presentation," your body would respond with feelings of anxiety and nervousness. These emotions could cause you to speak timidly, stumble over your words, or avoid eye contact. As a result, the presentation might not go well, reinforcing your belief that public speaking is embarrassing and confirming the very fear you started with.

I recently heard someone say, "I'm a great communicator. It's my partner who's the problem." Yet their emotions toward their partner were frustration and resentment. As a result, they started distancing themselves, shutting down communication, and even becoming borderline abusive. This led to more tension and misunderstandings, reinforcing their belief that the problem lay entirely with their partner's inability to communicate. The cycle fed itself, but it was clear that their actions were only worsening the situation.

If a thought can create your results, then why not change them?

I know I've shared this before, but it's worth repeating: before going into any situation, simply ask yourself, **"What do I want to create in this moment?"** This simple question will prompt a more empowering thought to arise, shifting your mindset. As a result, you'll approach the situation differently, leading to a completely different and more positive outcome than you might have previously expected.

Elevated Thoughts + Elevated Emotions + Elevated Actions = Elevated Results

How do you create transformation in all areas of your life that creates consistently elevated results?

If you want to break free and transform your life, you start by **elevating** your thoughts above your current level of emotions. With **elevated** thoughts, your body will generate **elevated** emotions. Almost naturally, you will want to choose **elevated** actions, which will produce an **elevated** experience in your life. And because you had an **elevated** result, this will create more elevated thoughts, and the cycle continues.

In this phase of The Creation Formula, you will learn and practice small and incremental changes to elevate your thoughts, feelings, and actions to create a new state of "being."

When you're "being" a new, greater version of yourself and operating at a new and higher level, you will experience the results of greater health, well-being, improved relationships, and greater wealth, the by-products of living an elevated life. You will feel yourself radiating with happiness, joy, confidence, and abundance.

Practices For Elevation

In the elevate phase, you will be introduced to a set of concepts and tiny habits that, over time, will produce long-lasting and transformational results in your life.

THE FOUR PILLARS OF A BALANCED LIFE

> *"Creating new things is infinitely easier than changing old things... If we focus on building the new, the old will ultimately go away."*
> **– Dr. Clayton Christensen**

While working as a software engineer for over three decades, I found it relatively easy to overfocus on work and let my life fall out of balance, wreaking havoc on other parts of my life. I remember working on projects until the early morning hours, only stopping when I was too exhausted to continue. The next day, I would drag myself out of bed, pounding down an energy drink to muster enough energy to start the day over. It was a cycle that seemed productive but came at a significant cost. Over time, I noticed the toll it took on my health, relationships, and overall well-being.

The Four Pillars of a Balanced Life

It wasn't until many years later, after becoming certified as a high-performance coach, that I adopted a new belief that being a high performer doesn't mean sacrificing other areas of life. **True, high performance isn't just about excelling at work; it's about thriving in all aspects of life.** I realized that the ultimate high performer is someone who achieves a balanced life, excelling not only in their career but also in their health, spiritual and mental well-being, relationships, and pursuits of wealth.

Those who lead this balanced lifestyle consistently practice habits that nurture four key areas of life. These key areas are like the pillars of a majestic temple. I refer to these as "The Four Pillars" of a balanced life: **Vitality (Body)**, **Insight (Being)**, **Harmony (Relationships)**, and **Purpose (Career/Business)**. By integrating small, simple habits in each pillar, you'll see dramatic improvements over time in these areas and experience positive ripple effects across all areas of your life.

The Pillar of Vitality focuses on the body (health and fitness). It's about establishing habits that elevate your physical well-being to a higher state. By developing a stronger and healthier body, you'll gain the power and energy to tackle life's challenges and show up confidently.

The Pillar of Insight focuses on mental, emotional, and spiritual well-being, encompassing practices that will give you a deeper understanding of yourself and greater emotional resilience. By fostering self-awareness and emotional intelligence, you will navigate life with clarity and calm.

The Pillar of Harmony focuses on fostering relationships with your spouse, partner, family, and friends. It involves cultivating a life of connection and compassion, building positive relationships that enhance your sense of belonging, and contributing to a fulfilling and enriched life.

The Pillar of Purpose is about aligning your actions with your core values and pursuing meaningful work. It involves discovering and following your passions, setting clear goals, and making a positive impact through your endeavors. This pillar gives you a sense of direction and fulfillment, guiding you toward a life driven by intention and purpose.

Through understanding and cultivating these pillars, I found a new path to "true" high performance, where success is measured not just by professional achievements but also by increased vitality, well-being, and fulfillment. I didn't have to sacrifice in one area to boost performance in the other, but what I discovered was when I put consistent effort into one pillar, it profoundly affected and reinforced another.

After consistently practicing habits in each of The Four Pillars over several years, I've achieved remarkable results in all areas of my life. I learned that by cultivating habits within these pillars, you can become a high performer not just temporarily but for a lifetime. This is because maintaining a balanced and fulfilled life prevents boredom and burnout, allowing you to sustain high performance and well-being over the long term.

Action

Take a moment to journal the following:

- What pillar of your life do you need to elevate the most?
- What do you tell yourself about this pillar, and how does it make you feel?
- When you feel the way you do, what actions do you take or fail to take?

SYSTEM THINKING VERSUS LINEAR THINKING

> "Business and human endeavors are systems...we tend to focus on snapshots of isolated parts of the system. And wonder why our deepest problems never get solved."
> **– Peter Senge**

From a young age, much of our learning was through cause and effect, which shaped our thinking about life into a linear approach. When we learned how to walk, we would stand and then fall, then try again, making attempt after attempt until we finally learned to stand and walk. We learned cause-and-effect thinking because of the immediate feedback, and we were able to quickly make the necessary adjustments and succeed.

System Thinking Versus Linear Thinking

If you've ever grabbed the handle of a hot pan on the stove and burned your hand, there was immediate feedback to let you know not to do that again without a hot pad. If you ever spent hours preparing for a hard exam and you ended up scoring well, you learned that hard work and preparation pays off.

Peter Senge's book *The Fifth Discipline* describes linear thinking and systems thinking. He shows how linear thinking is a more traditional and straightforward approach to thinking, where problems are broken down into separate components and tackled step-by-step. This is the approach that most of us take in our daily lives.

Systems thinking is a holistic approach to analysis that focuses on the way that a system's constituent parts interrelate and how systems work overtime and within the context of larger systems. It emphasizes understanding the whole rather than just individual components. In systems thinking, the focus is on patterns and interdependencies, recognizing that actions and outcomes are often the result of complex and dynamic interactions. This approach encourages looking at problems from multiple perspectives and considering long-term consequences and feedback loops.

Although *The Fifth Discipline* was geared toward business and its systems, I realized how **this is a missing link in our thinking regarding our personal lives**. If we could start thinking about our lives in a holistic systems thinking approach where The Four

Pillars are the components of a larger system, which, in fact, they are, we might start being more balanced rather than hyperfocused in one area and not the other.

For example, how can not taking care of my fitness affect my income? Or my relationships?

When I was younger, I didn't see the consequences of lack of exercise because my energy was high. I could work easily late into the night, but as I started getting older, it became very apparent that the lack of exercise diminished my energy and health. With less energy, I couldn't perform as well in my career; I couldn't sit in my office chair very long without getting a sore back. And the back pain would drain the life out of me and destroy my motivation to work hard. I would show up to meetings, but it probably looked like I just rolled out of bed. My physical presence looked like I didn't take care of myself, with tired eyes and my belly busting out over my jeans.

When I arrived home from work, I was tired and exhausted and didn't feel like doing much except watching TV or playing video games late into the night. My relationships suffered because I suffered.

However, things turned around when I started a daily exercise program that increased my energy levels and overall physical fitness which allowed me to do my job without being exhausted. I could show up to meetings at work feeling powerful and with energy surging through my body. Showing up for my family became much easier because I had the energy to be present.

We are not used to thinking about the interdependencies that each pillar has on the other, but by studying those who are living their lives at the highest level, they understand this concept and have habits and routines in place to live the life they designed.

When you begin to recognize the dynamic interactions between The Four Pillars of your life, you'll observe clear evidence that enhancing one pillar indeed strengthens them all. Putting positive, vibrant energy into each component of the system elevates the entire system.

Action

Take a few minutes to answer the following questions:

- When you think about the pillars of vitality, insight, harmony, or purpose, how does each one affect the other?
- In your life, how does the pillar that you described in the previous chapter affect the other areas of your life?
- What would happen to the other pillars if you strengthened the one that is the weakest?

HABITS THAT BUILD THE FOUR PILLARS

> "We are what we repeatedly do. Excellence, then, is not an act but a habit."
> **– Aristotle**

Before implementing the habits described in the expansion phase, you would have found a divorced, broken, depressed, and out-of-shape man. My relationships with my children were decimated, and I could barely show up to work. A decision to commit myself to a program that required me to get up every morning and follow a daily routine that would lift and energize me changed my life forever. In addition, I hired a success coach, and over the course of several months, I was able to transform my life across all four pillars.

I got up every morning and proceeded to do the work. It didn't take long for me to feel the light and energy returning to my life. I began to feel more energized and vibrant in spirit. Depression and anxiety lifted, and I began to feel greater hope, more joy, and fulfillment in my life. Over time, I was able to repair my relationships with all my children.

I believe my youngest son got the most neglect after my wife passed away because I dragged him through two failed marriages, and I was barely coping with my own pain and anguish. He was only thirteen when she passed, and he was depressed and struggling with feeling any emotions at all. He seemed to have suppressed them deeply after his mother's passing. But one day, as he saw me doing my daily routine, he asked, "Dad, can I come to the gym with you?" I am so grateful he reached out and asked because I thought he would have never considered it.

We got to spend some good quality time together at the gym every morning before work. I could see his spirits lifting, and he was feeling more energetic. We had some good talks about his mom and the challenges of life. I was able to let him know how sorry I was about the way things had gone in the years after his mother's passing.

Slowly, the emotions started to return to where he could feel again, and about the time I was preparing myself to meet an incredible woman who is my wife today, my son also met a beautiful young lady to whom he is happily married.

I look back on those years and see how hard life was then, but the most valuable thing in our lives is our precious relationships. A huge revelation for me was how much influence for the good we have on each other. The change in my son didn't occur by harping at him to join in with me on my routines even though I knew it would benefit him; it was by me just getting up every day and doing the work to change myself.

It was proof enough that everything around us changes when we change. One of my favorite things to say to others is, **"When the tide rises, all of the boats in the harbor rise. Be the tide and rise."**

"When we change the way we look at things, the things we look at change."
– Dr. Wayne Dyer

I strongly believe that **if you want to create massive change in your life, the only thing that must change is you.** When you commit and consistently work to make the changes necessary to transform your life, you will experience changes, often dramatic, in all four pillars of your life. Your influence will be felt all around, and you will become a leader and an example of what is possible.

Let's start elevating our lives by introducing the first habit that will create dramatic changes and help us elevate our being to a new and higher state.

Action

Take a few minutes to answer these questions:

- What is the biggest challenge you currently face in The Four Pillars (health & fitness, mental & spiritual well-being, relationships, career & income)?
- What would the ideal outcome look like in each of these areas?

ELEVATE THE PILLAR OF VITALITY

> *"Take care of your body. It's the only place you have to live."*
> **– Jim Rohn**

Earlier, I shared how I set a tiny goal to simply walk through the gym doors every day. I wanted to make the goal incredibly simple and easy. I made this decision after having suffered from depression for most of my adult life. I already knew from experience that exercise was beneficial, but for some reason, that day, I was reading an article that said how exercise produced more natural drugs and was more effective than any antidepressant on the market to help with depression. That day, after reading that article, I decided to set the goal of just walking through those doors every day. And now, several years later, I don't even have to set an alarm because my body just knows it's time to get out of bed and head to the gym.

I don't even give it a second thought, and it's a habit that will benefit me for years.

Exercise

Exercise isn't just about physical fitness—it's the cornerstone of a healthy and fulfilling life, impacting every aspect of your well-being. As one of The Four Pillars, regular physical activity offers a wealth of benefits that extend far beyond maintaining a healthy weight or building muscle. Exercise strengthens your cardiovascular system, reduces the risk of chronic diseases like heart disease and diabetes, and boosts your immune system, making your body more resilient against illnesses. It's also vital for keeping your bones and joints healthy, which becomes increasingly important as we age.

But the benefits of exercise don't stop at the physical level. When you think about The Four Pillars as an interconnected system, exercise plays a crucial role in enhancing your mental, spiritual, and emotional well-being. Regular physical activity has been proven to reduce symptoms of anxiety and depression, thanks to the natural "feel-good" endorphins released during exercise. This not only lifts your mood but also promotes a greater sense of overall well-being.

Exercise also sharpens your mind, improving cognitive function, memory, and productivity. It boosts your energy levels and improves sleep quality, making you more effective in all areas of your life. When you consider how the pillars interact, it's clear that exercise enhances performance across the board, helping you excel in each of The Four Pillars.

On a spiritual level, exercise can serve as a form of moving meditation, offering a chance to connect with yourself, reduce stress, and cultivate mindfulness. By incorporating regular exercise into your life, you're not just elevating your physical health but also nurturing your mental, emotional, and spiritual well-being. This holistic approach creates a harmonious balance that supports a thriving, vibrant life.

Why wait? Start by making a tiny goal to exercise and experience its transformative power in all aspects of your life.

Activity

Choose an activity you enjoy and commit to doing it for at least ten minutes daily.

If you don't already have this as a habit and you are ready to fully commit, I want you to pull out your phone and set an alarm. Just a few minutes a day at the right time will give you that extra boost you might be looking for.

ELEVATE THE PILLAR OF INSIGHT

> *"All of humanity's problems stem from man's inability to sit quietly in a room alone."*
> **– Blaise Pascal**

In your journey to create a new reality for your life, a key step to elevating yourself involves nurturing and enhancing the pillar of Insight (being): your mental, spiritual, and emotional well-being. By cultivating a healthy mind, a deep spiritual connection, and emotional intelligence, you will create a new elevated level of "being."

We could cover many great habits here, but I just want to emphasize a couple of easy-to-perform habits that encompass all three phases: Expand, Elevate, and Envision.

They are meditation and journaling. This type of journaling isn't the traditional type, so let me explain each in some detail.

Meditation

Meditation is one of my favorite practices in the realm of personal development because of its profound benefits for health and mental, spiritual, and emotional well-being. Even a short session always brings me a great amount of peace and joy.

When I first started meditating, I was suffering mentally and emotionally, and I was dealing with extreme stress and high blood pressure. And over just a couple of months, I saw drastic changes in my stress levels and greater emotional resilience. And I experienced amazing results in decreasing my blood pressure without any medication. I know from my personal life the power of this simple practice.

In recent years, there has been a surge in research, with over 4,000 studies conducted on the benefits of meditation as a valuable practice for enhancing well-being. A Google Scholar search for the benefits of meditation returned over 594,000 results.

Are you overwhelmed by stress, struggling to focus, or searching for deeper meaning in life?

Meditation might just be the solution you're looking for. This simple yet powerful practice offers a wide range of health benefits that can transform your **mental**, **physical**, and **spiritual well-being**.

Imagine reducing stress and anxiety with just a few minutes of daily practice. Meditation lowers cortisol levels, the hormone responsible for stress, helping you manage anxiety and depression more effectively. It sharpens your focus and enhances cognitive clarity, making it easier to navigate life's challenges with a calm, centered mind.

Physically, meditation has been shown to lower blood pressure, improve heart health, and even boost your immune system, making you more resilient to illness. It promotes better sleep by quieting your mind, leading to more restful, restorative nights.

Meditation doesn't just benefit your body—it profoundly impacts your mind and spirit. By quieting the constant chatter of the "monkey mind," meditation allows you to cultivate mindfulness and stay fully present in the moment. As you become more aware of your thoughts and emotions, you'll gain greater clarity and resilience, enabling you to respond to life's challenges with grace. Over time, this practice can improve your cognitive function, enhance your concentration, and give you a balanced perspective on life's ups and downs.

Spiritually, meditation serves as a gateway to deeper self-awareness and a connection with God or your higher self. Think of prayer as speaking to God and meditation as listening. This introspective practice creates a space for you to connect with your spirit, leading to a profound sense of inner peace and contentment. It can open you to spiritual experiences, such as a sense of unity with all existence or a deep understanding of your purpose in life.

Emotionally, meditation provides a sanctuary where you can process and release pent-up emotions. It teaches you to observe your feelings without getting overwhelmed, promoting emotional stability and maturity. As you meditate, you'll develop a compassionate attitude toward yourself and others, enhancing your relationships and allowing you to navigate life's challenges with patience and kindness.

Incorporating meditation into your daily routine nurtures a balanced emotional state, helping you experience more joy, gratitude, and overall well-being. It's a powerful tool for anyone looking to improve their quality of life, deepen their spiritual connection, and find peace in a chaotic world.

Are you ready to give it a try?

Your mind, body, and spirit will thank you.

Journaling

I gained some of the greatest insights and lessons in life through journaling as a daily activity. This is a very specific type of journaling used in the Expansion phase to find the hidden programming that is limiting your life and keeping you stuck.

Are you constantly overwhelmed by the endless stream of thoughts racing through your mind? Or do you struggle with finding clarity amid the chaos?

Consider a prompt-based transformative style of journaling—not the traditional kind that merely documents your life's events, but a deeper, more introspective form of journaling. This type of journaling is designed to help you process emotions, engage in deep self-reflection, and rewrite the internal programming that may be holding you back. It's about creating new stories, beliefs, and rules that align with the life you truly want to live.

Journaling allows you to take the constant hamster wheel of thoughts out of your head and put them on paper. When you write, your brain naturally slows down, allowing you to process your thoughts more effectively. This act of slowing down provides a safe outlet for expressing and releasing pent-up emotions. It helps you identify and understand the feelings you're experiencing and uncovers the underlying stories that shape them. By gaining this insight, you can begin to reframe your thoughts and rewrite the programming that no longer serves you.

Beyond emotional release, journaling is a powerful tool for problem-solving and personal growth. When you're faced with challenges, writing about your dilemmas helps you to organize your thoughts, explore different perspectives, and often discover solutions that were previously hidden. This practice not only nurtures mindfulness and presence, helping you stay grounded and centered, but it also promotes emotional healing and resilience. Through the simple act of writing, you can gain profound lessons and revelations that lead to lasting change and a deeper understanding of yourself.

If you're looking to break free from the mental clutter and create a new reality for your life, journaling is an invaluable tool that can help you achieve the clarity, peace, and growth you desire.

Activity

I. Meditation

There are many different forms of meditation, each offering unique approaches and benefits. Take some time to explore the various forms of meditation and pick one that suits you best. I prefer a mix of guided, mantra, and sound-based meditations with mindfulness practices.

I would like to share with you the "I Love Myself" meditation that I created specifically to heal my emotional wounds. It transformed my life and many others. I've included it as a supplement to this book. To download, go to the website at e3blueprint.com/bookbonus

Do this meditation daily, and you will notice a greater sense of well-being and self-love, less stress and anxiety, and greater emotional resiliency toward things that are out of your control.

II. Journaling

Journaling can be done at any time of the day, but it should be done for at least a few minutes daily.

Get the detailed phase 1 journaling prompts at e3blueprint.com/bookbonus.

ELEVATE THE PILLAR OF HARMONY

> *"Connection is why we're here; it is what gives purpose and meaning to our lives."*
> **– Brené Brown**

There was a time in my life after my wife passed away, and my attempts at remarriage fell apart, when I found myself utterly alone and devastated. The weight of those failed relationships, along with my own downward spiral, took a heavy toll on my connection with my children. It felt like all the pain and negativity had pushed them away, and I could hardly blame them. I had become a walking disaster, and they wanted nothing to do with me.

It wasn't until after I had decided to go all-in on these habits that miracles started to happen. I felt the shift in me and the surge of positive energy that gave me the lift I needed to create a better life. I healed myself from the inside, rewriting old programming and letting go of past failures and mistakes. Letting go of the regret and shame of the failures of my life. In doing so, my life began to transform, and those around me felt it and were lifted with me.

When your relationships are a mess, eventually, they will cause everything else to come burning down around you. It's just a matter of time before you self-implode and find yourself in a pit of despair. I have seen it happen to many people.

You have the choice to change it all and make a difference in your life and in the lives of those around you. In Bronnie Ware's book *The Top Five Regrets of the Dying: A Life Transformed by the Dearly Departing*, two of the top five regrets were about relationships. One regret was, "I wish I hadn't worked so hard." And another was, "I wish I had stayed in touch with my friends." The things we regret the most aren't making more money or being ultra-successful in business but spending more time with family and friends and not being afraid to live the life we want.

Building Connections

Building a connection is the first step toward cultivating a great relationship, one that leads to a fulfilling and joyful life. Strong relationships fulfill your need for belonging and support, significantly enhancing your emotional and mental well-being.

Building your connection with your spouse fosters trust, intimacy, and mutual respect, helping you navigate the maze of life together. Connecting with your children will build those strong familial ties that create a foundation for their emotional development and boost their confidence in handling life's challenges.

Connecting with friends will provide you with a network of emotional strength and shared experiences. I know for certain how important friendships were to me during the many years of suffering and hardship. Friends allow for the opportunity to see new perspectives and can support your personal growth.

Investing in your relationships will enrich your life and make them a crucial element of overall happiness and satisfaction.

Are you ready to start building stronger connections today?

Your future self will thank you.

Activity

Uncertainty about how to build strong relationships can discourage many people from trying anything.

How about we make this easy to do so that you can start building strong connections?

Every day, pick two people to make a connection with. If you are married or in a relationship, your spouse or partner is the first. If you have children, the second pick is one of your children, and if you have no children, then the second one can be extended family or friends. Of course, you can choose more than two, but the idea is to build a new simple habit that is small and easy to do. Once established, you can add more. If you have more than one child, alternate between them.

The idea is to connect meaningfully with the receiver, sending them a message of love and appreciation or uniquely honoring them.

- Put a note on a Post-it note and leave it on the bathroom mirror or their bedroom door.
- Send a text message or email of appreciation or honoring something they have done in the past.
- A quick FaceTime with your child is always a fun surprise.
- A quick phone call to let someone know you are thinking of them.
- Set a lunch date with an old friend.

There are many ways to do this, but the idea is to keep it simple so you can build the habit of connecting daily. Just letting someone know how much you are grateful for them opens their hearts and knocks down old barriers of resentment and anger and opens their hearts to receive your love.

You may think this whole exercise is more about the person you are directing the message to, but in reality, you will be the benefactor of the giving because it will change you and your heart. After doing this consistently over a short time, you will show up as a changed person.

ELEVATE THE PILLAR OF PURPOSE

> "Success is not the key to happiness. Happiness is the key to success. If you love what you are doing, you will be successful."
> — **Albert Schweitzer**

It seems that over the last few years, there has been a lot of attention put on finding your gifts and your true purpose in life. I even got caught up in trying to figure out what my true purpose was and struggled in defining it.

Quotes like this from Buddha, "Your purpose in life is to find your purpose and give your whole heart and soul to it," get everyone caught up in the frenzy of trying to figure out their purpose.

What if your purpose is what you decide it to be? What if you decide that you want to change your purpose multiple times in your lifetime?

You are the creator of your life, and so I find the answer you choose is entirely up to you. You get to decide and choose what you want to do in this life. Whether you feel a desire to become a doctor, engineer, pilot, electrician, politician, or entrepreneur or choose from thousands of different careers, it is entirely up to you.

The Pillar of Purpose is your choice of how to create your income, and the power is all on you to decide where to focus your energy. If you want to elevate yourself to be the best in your chosen career, building a habit of continuous learning will lift you to the top. The greater the value you can create for others, the greater the demand for your talents.

Growth In Daily Learning

The top 1 percent are success-oriented individuals who never stop learning. They constantly seek out new knowledge, skills, and experiences to stay ahead of the curve. Whether through formal education, reading, mentorship, or hands-on experience, they are committed to personal and professional growth, which enables them to adapt to changes and capitalize on new opportunities.

Incorporating daily learning into your routine can be a transformative practice that profoundly enriches your life. By dedicating just a small portion of your day to acquiring new knowledge or honing a skill, you keep your mind sharp, expand your horizons, and cultivate a sense of purpose.

Over the last several years, I have had the opportunity to learn from the best books, programs, and courses. These have not only given me the confidence to perform at the highest level but also the ability to lead and elevate others. What started out as a small habit of reading a few minutes a day has turned into a habit of reading one book a week over the last several years.

By committing to just a little bit of learning each day, you'll sharpen your mind, boost your creativity, and become a more effective problem-solver. You'll find yourself more confident, ready to tackle challenges, and seize the opportunities that come your way.

But the benefits don't stop there. Daily learning also nurtures your emotional and mental well-being, bringing a deep sense of fulfillment and joy. It expands your worldview, helping you connect with others and understand different perspectives. Whether you're aiming to advance in your career, build stronger relationships, or find greater meaning in life, making learning a daily habit is the key to unlocking your potential. Invest in yourself through daily learning and watch as it transforms not just your knowledge but your entire life.

Activity

Start a daily habit of learning by simply taking ten minutes a day to learn something new.

START A POWERFUL DAY

> *"It's not what we do once in a while that shapes our lives, but what we do consistently."*
> **– Tony Robbins**

Starting your day with powerful habits that elevate your mood sets you up to win every single day. For me, beginning each morning with routines that empower me, lift my spirit, and prepare me emotionally and mentally for the day ahead has been truly life-changing.

Reflecting on the days when I used to drag myself out of bed and rely on energy drinks just to get through the morning, the difference between who I was then and who I am today is remarkable. Now, I wake up around 5 a.m. every morning without an alarm. My mind and body know what to do next with exactness—there's no internal debate about how to start my day.

This is a far cry from someone who used to say, "I'm a night person; I can't get up early."

> "How you start your day determines how you create your life."
> **– Hal Elrod**

One of the books that really reinforced this transformation is *The Miracle Morning* by Hal Elrod. He emphasizes the importance of starting the day with intention, focus, and positivity. By adopting a morning routine, you set yourself up for success and unlock your full potential.

> "You do not rise to the level of your goals. You fall to the level of your systems."
> **– James Clear**

Similarly, in *Atomic Habits*, James Clear argues that instead of trying to overhaul your life with drastic changes, focusing on small, consistent habits can lead to significant and sustainable results over time. His approach emphasizes creating a system that, when practiced consistently, gradually builds momentum, replacing negative habits with positive ones and leading to lasting transformation.

When building and maintaining The Four Pillars, you can incorporate any number of habits, but the key is to start with simple, easy-to-do routines that lay the foundation for future growth. Every day you wake up is a new opportunity to transform yourself, even if it's just a small step forward. Over the course of a few months, you'll look back and see a measurable difference in who you've become.

Ultimately, the choice is yours to establish new powerful habits to elevate yourself to a higher level of well-being and performance. By consistently nurturing The Four Pillars, you set the stage for success in every aspect of your life. Small, intentional steps each day will build the resilience, clarity, and energy you need to face challenges head-on and achieve your dreams. Elevating yourself through your daily routines isn't just about feeling better in the moment—it's about raising your frequency, increasing your energy, building the foundation for long-term success, and thriving in all that you do.

THE JOURNEY OF ELEVATION

> *"Everything is energy and that's all there is to it. Match the frequency of the reality you want and you cannot help but get that reality. It can be no other way. This is not philosophy. This is physics."*
> **– Albert Einstein**

In my journey to discover how to be a creator of my life, I found that elevating my life to a new level required a daily commitment to a new approach in life. I could not just keep thinking, feeling, and doing the same old things and expect a different result. To create something new, things had to change. I had to create daily practices and routines that would elevate me to a new level of mind and body. To think differently, I needed new input, and to feel different, I needed to practice things that would allow my body to feel greater energy and more empowering feelings and emotions.

In Search of The Creation Formula

In the journey to be the creator of your life, you must elevate yourself in a systematic approach to produce the fruits you desire. Leveling up your energy is a must since you are an energetic being.

Think about it: You're made up of 99.99999 percent energy and a tiny fraction of matter. Your heart and mind are constantly broadcasting your thoughts and feelings out into the world, like a radio station sending out a signal. That energy shapes everything around you—your experiences, relationships, and reality.

This isn't just some abstract concept. The way you think and feel at any moment creates your "state of being," and that state drives your actions. When you consciously elevate your state of being, you start making choices that align with the life you truly want. You're not just reacting to life; **you're shaping it, molding it into the reality you desire.**

Every single day, the habits you choose either lift you or hold you back. When you elevate yourself through small, consistent actions, you raise your energy, impacting your Four Pillars—Vitality, Insight, Harmony, and Purpose. The energy you send into the world attracts experiences that match that frequency. When your thoughts, feelings, and actions align with your highest self, you will attract to you the life you've always dreamed of.

This journey of elevation isn't just a nice-to-have—it's essential. It's the path to becoming the greatest version of yourself. You build momentum that transforms your life by taking small, powerful steps

The Journey of Elevation

each day. These tiny habits are the building blocks to creating a system for yourself to bring about transformation, leading you to a joyful, purpose-filled life.

But here's the thing: elevation isn't a one-time deal. It's a daily choice, a commitment to rise above the ordinary and to step into your true potential. Each day is a fresh opportunity to elevate your life, align with your highest self, and create the future you've always envisioned.

So, keep going. Don't stop now. The power to shape your life is in your hands, and you've only begun to tap into it. Keep elevating, keep growing, and keep reaching for the extraordinary. This is your life, and you have the power to make it truly magnificent. The journey doesn't end here—it's just getting started.

PHASE 3
ENVISION

> *"You can't depend on your eyes when your imagination is out of focus."*
> **– Mark Twain**

Now that we've laid the foundation of The Creation Formula by expanding our consciousness and elevating our energy and state of being, it's time to turn our attention "forward" to the next phase of the formula, the **Envision** phase. This phase is the most exciting part of the entire equation; it is about envisioning a powerful, uplifting future, a future you want to create.

Envisioning isn't just about daydreaming or wishful thinking—it's about clearly defining the life you want and aligning your energy, thoughts, and actions to bring that vision to life. In the **Expansion** phase, we learned to see life with new perspectives and learned

Phase 3: Envision

the power of the reframe in which we have the ability to define a new frame in which we can view our life. With the ability to see life through a new lens and reframe any obstacle into a lesson, you can start to craft a compelling future **that excites you, challenges you, and pulls you forward.**

In the **Elevate** phase, you learned that you must elevate yourself to a new energy to create something new. We are what we repeatedly do, and the systems we create define who we become. With a new level of energy, the result must be transformation, and science proves it. The next phase will bring even more energy and excitement to the equation.

In the **Envision** phase, **we'll explore how to harness the power of your imagination to create a vision so strong that it becomes a driving force in your life.** We'll dive into the techniques and practices that will help you see beyond your current reality and step into the future you desire with clarity and confidence.

You've already started creating a new future by expanding your consciousness and elevating yourself to a higher state of being. Now it's time to direct your expanded and elevated self toward a vision of your future that might feel impossible in your present state, but what you will learn is how to make the impossible possible. This is where the magic happens—where the life you've always dreamed of begins to take shape, and you become the conscious creator of your destiny.

Get ready to dream big, push the boundaries of what you believe is possible, and start manifesting the future you've always wanted. **The Envision phase is where your dreams begin to turn into reality.**

Let's step into this next chapter with enthusiasm and intention to be the creator of your new reality.

Your future is waiting.

LOOKING FORWARD TO THE FUTURE

> *"The best way to predict the future is to create it."*
> **— Peter Drucker**

By the fall of 2017, I had hit a new low. I was now dealing with the fallout from a second failed marriage after losing my wife in 2011. My relationships with my children were in ruins, and I was barely hanging on to my job. It felt like I was trapped in a deep, dark pit, with the walls closing in and the light getting dimmer by the day. The gut-wrenching pain of loss weighed heavily on me, and waves of guilt and shame would flood over me, reminding me of the mistakes I'd made since losing my late wife, Amy.

To make matters worse, my daughter informed me that her little family was moving away to her husband's home state of Florida. Around the same time, my oldest son had stopped talking to me altogether. I'm not sharing this to cast any blame on my children but to show how negative energy can push people away, even when we're silently begging for them to come closer. I needed those who were close to me to come nearer, but the opposite happened; it repelled them and left me feeling more isolated and depressed than ever before. The weight of despair and hopelessness was crushing, and I couldn't see a way out.

Being in that state and knowing that feeling of hopelessness and despair helped me understand why it is so easy for people to give up on life and lose all hope for the future. I often reflect on my best friend Joe, who took his life, and how he, too, must have lost all hope. I have always wished I could have done more to make a difference in his life so he would still be here today. One of the many reasons I am sharing this book is to bring hope to as many as possible that our future hasn't been written yet, and we are the creators of that future. And we do have a say in what kind of future is created. As the creator of your future, it's time to learn to dream again and dream as big as your heart desires.

During the fall of that same year, I signed up for a personal development conference, and my transformation began. In 2017, I began my journey to heal the wounds of my past and do the work to repair my life. But what got it all started was realizing there was hope for a brighter future, that I could regain control of my own ship and be the captain once again.

The future is far brighter and more expansive than we often allow ourselves to believe. One of the biggest mistakes we make as we get older is that our ability to dream and imagine begins to fade. We get caught up in the routine, living inside a false reality—"the matrix" of our lives—and we stop believing we have the power to shape it. We lose sight of our ability to create the outcomes we truly desire.

I have discovered that the more I can dream and hope about the future, the more I am compelled to take action to make it a reality.

I discovered that even in the darkest moments, renewal is possible. There is a strength and resilience that innately resides deep inside us. We have this ability to overcome the most challenging adversities. And although it may feel like everything is burning down around you, like a phoenix rising from the ashes, you can be reborn, renewed, rise up, stronger, wiser, and more resilient than before. We have the ability to rebuild our lives, transforming our pain into a source of power and hope for a brighter future.

Embracing God and having faith in Him, we realize that no matter how intense the despair, there is always a chance to rise again. This realization gave me the strength to move forward, knowing that even in my most broken state, I could be reborn and start anew.

There is a growing body of research in neuroscience and psychology that suggests that it is no longer our past traumas that are affecting our future, but rather, it is whether or not we have compelling goals for our future. The research suggests that **we are pulled forward into the future by our goals and purpose,**

and the quality of our life in the present directly correlates with our connection with our future self.

When we look to the future with hope, it creates a feeling of optimism and possibility. Those feelings allow us to see life with a new perspective that can inspire peace and confidence within us and allow us to face our challenges with strength and resilience. It can give us a deep sense of purpose and motivation to look forward to the future.

Any time in my life when I have found myself stuck, bored, tired, or lacking the motivation to move forward, I discovered that I hadn't updated my goals or had lost the vision of my purpose for a time, which drained the energy out of having any compelling future.

> *"The only way to make your present better is by making your future bigger."*
> **– Dan Sullivan**

When I became a hypnotherapist, one of the techniques we learned was future pacing. This technique helps clients utilize all their senses to see, hear, feel, and vividly experience a compelling future. When this technique is performed, you can't help but walk away from the session feeling happy, uplifted, and drawn toward this new future that you have envisioned for yourself.

One of my heroes is my father. I already shared how he lost his business and had to start over at the age of fifty-three. After that devastating period in his life, I watched this man look to the future time and time again. He took repeated actions to design his life the way he wanted it. The reason he worked hard in life was so he could be with family and play hard.

He loved to play, so he was always out fishing, camping, hunting, playing racquetball, tennis, golf, skiing, or anything outdoors. He loved life, and he loved trying to include you in it with him.

I have watched him grow into his later years, and his desire to get out and do things didn't diminish until his last couple of months of life. I always knew that the end would be near for my father when he put away his golf clubs. However, the lessons of life he has taught me are invaluable, and his drive to live a full and beautiful life shows me how important it is to look to the future with hope and always have a dream. My father battled cancer for several years, but you would never have known because his desire to live life and dream big kept him alive a lot longer than any of his doctors had predicted.

Having a dream for the future pulls us forward toward it. In the book *Man's Search for Meaning*, Viktor Frankl stated, **"Those who have a 'why' to live, can bear with almost any 'how.'"** Having a sense of purpose, a "why," was not only crucial for enduring and overcoming suffering, but from Frankl's experience in concentration camps during the Holocaust, he observed that prisoners who lost their sense of purpose or meaning in life were more likely to succumb to despair and death. Frankl said, "The moment a man ceases to see meaning in his life, he retreats into a state of mere existence and, in the end, succumbs to physical and mental decay."

By looking into the future and connecting with your future self, you will take control of your destiny and become the creator of your life, no longer the victim of circumstances.

Looking forward will help you shift your focus from the broken recordings of the past and transform yourself in a way that will fill your life with purpose, fulfillment, and success.

Action

Take a few minutes to journal the following questions:

- How critical is it for you to find and maintain a sense of meaning or purpose?
- How could looking toward the future with hope create change in your life?

CRAFTING A CRYSTAL-CLEAR VISION

> *"All things are created twice; first mentally, then physically. The key to creativity is to begin with the end in mind, with a vision and a blueprint of the desired result."*
> **– Steven R. Covey**

One of the greatest exercises you can do for yourself is to get clear on your future self. The book *Breaking the Habit of Being Yourself* refers to quantum creating, where there is a future version of yourself that already exists as a possibility in the quantum field that already has all that you ever need, want, or desire. This future version of you is smarter, wiser, more emotionally resilient, and has already walked the path to where you are going. Your future self is just waiting to be observed by you.

In Search of The Creation Formula

Dr. Dispenza states, "If your mind can influence the appearance of an electron, then theoretically, it can influence the appearance of any possibility." This simply means that what I focus on is what I create. If your brain is constantly flooded with thoughts that create feelings of anxiety and worry, then there is a high probability that you will create negative outcomes in your life. If your thoughts are stuck in the past, then there is a good chance you are feeling depressed and sad most of the time, and if I were to ask you about your future goals or dreams, it may have been a while since that has been your focus.

That feeling of being lost or stuck in life comes when there are no goals to draw your attention forward. When there is a lack of a clear vision for your future, it is very hard to hope and believe that your life can be any better than it is in the present. A clear vision of what you want for your future self will give you a sense of direction and purpose.

Defining your future self is not about predicting who you will be but deciding who you want to become. It's a deliberate act of creation in your mind, and you sculpt the person you aspire to become.

The latest research shows that the more connected you are with your future self, the wiser your decisions will be in the present. And if you spend more time thinking about your future self, you will be more likely to invest in yourself.

In his book *Be Your Future Self Now*, Dr. Benjamin Hardy describes how the brain is like a "prediction machine."

When we start with what we want in the future, our brain automatically wants to work backward to help us think and act from the goal. He states, "The clearer you are on where you want to go, the less distracted you'll be by endless options."

Envisioning your future will help you build a connection with your future self, and **the quality of that connection you have with your future self will determine the quality of your life and behaviors in the present**.

When disconnected from our future selves, we tend to opt for the things in life that give us immediate gratification. We want that immediate dopamine hit, like when we sit and scroll through social media or binge-watch our favorite shows. We tend to stay up late because we think our future selves don't need sleep, and we are dragging ourselves out of bed the next day. We don't invest in our retirement because we have no sense of connection to our future self, and we don't even consider that our future self needs money in the future.

The clearer and more connected you are with your future self, the better you will be in the present. Current research shows that it is not the past that drives our current behaviors but our future goals.

The more connected you are with your future self, the clearer your direction will be. The more connected you are the wiser the decisions and choices you will make that will affect your results in life. The more connected you are with your future self, the more inspired you will be to innovate and find new solutions, and you will grow in new ways that were not previously considered.

Being connected to your future self will act like a magnet, pulling you into the future and guiding your actions. **Without a connection with your future self, you might wander aimlessly; with a connection, you will be drawn forward with purpose and clarity.**

A deeper connection with your future self will help promote thoughts, emotions, and actions more aligned with your desired outcomes. This alignment ensures that the energy you put out into the world is consistent with the future you want to create, increasing the likelihood of manifesting that vision.

A Time Capsule from The Future

Have you heard of the YouTube superstar Jimmy Donaldson, better known as MrBeast? When Jimmy was in high school, he recorded several videos in which he spoke about his future self. He recorded each one as if he were six months, twelve months, five years, and ten years into the future. They lasted about two minutes each. In these videos, he had an intimate and authentic conversation with his future self. He expressed his hopes and desires and then published them to be released on YouTube in the future.

In October 2020, when MrBeast's five-year video "Hi Me in Five Years" went live, he said, "Dude, If I don't have a million subscribers when you see this video, my entire life has been a failure." When his video went live, from "MrBeast World Record Numbers," there were over 44 million subscribers and over 7 billion views on his channel, and he had over 22 million in earnings. He didn't just reach his dream, he crushed it and, since then, has become the most-subscribed channel on YouTube with over 313 million subscribers.

Creating a vision for your future self is powerful. Let's take some time to create a time capsule of your own. It can be a note jotted down on a Post-it, a formal letter to yourself, or a video. Take the time to create something to your future self.

Action

There are a couple of different approaches to connecting to your future self. One is to write a letter to your future self, and the other is to write a letter from your future self.

When writing a letter to your future self, clarify how you see yourself. This will bring greater clarity and power into your present. Take some time now to write a letter. Go to e3blueprint.com/bookbonus for further details on how to do this.

DREAMING BIG, CREATING BIGGER

> *"Impossible is just a big word thrown around by small men who find it easier to live in the world they've been given than to explore the power they have to change it. Impossible is not a fact. It's an opinion. Impossible is not a declaration. It's a dare. Impossible is potential. Impossible is temporary. Impossible is nothing."*
> **– Muhammad Ali**

Now that you are looking toward the future with clarity, hope, and greater purpose, the next step to build a bigger, brighter, bolder future self is to start dreaming even bigger. It will help you move toward a new version of yourself that is stronger, more vibrant, and more resilient.

I ran across a leading coach and motivational speaker, Florencia Andres, who worked with star athletes to level up their game. One of the things she did was ask them to "dream the impossible." When they were in a slump and struggling with success, she had them dream bigger than they had done before. This ignited a fire within them to go to the next level and achieve extraordinary results.

If superstars need help leveling up their mindset to get to the next level, how much do you think everyone else needs it, too?

Are you the captain of your ship of life? Or has your crew mutinied and taken over?

Are you ready to gain greater control?

The best way to create massive energy and motivation is to start to dream big again. You are now empowered to expand your mind and reframe your past to move past the old stumbling blocks that used to hold you back.

Let's reactivate that creative side of your incredible brain and start to imagine a bigger and bolder life. When I started to dream again and set the intention that I would take back my life and become the creator of my life, evidence of my desire started to show up all around me.

Research has shown that the older we get, the less we activate our imagination, so it makes sense that we would transform less. The good news is that we must reactivate this part of the brain and start dreaming again.

By allowing yourself to imagine the future you want, you will activate a part of you that may have been dormant or suppressed. It will awaken you to feel alive again and motivated to move forward. When you begin to imagine a bigger and brighter future, this will help define your "why," the clearer and more defined you can imagine it, the greater the drive will become.

10X Your Future

Are you ready to 10x your future? You're probably saying, "What, are you crazy? You just asked me to start dreaming, and now you want me to 10X my future?"

It's not as crazy as you might think. Let me explain.

From a young age, I was taught at school and in sports that to improve or get better at something, I had to define and set a goal to improve my performance. Later in my career, it became common practice to set yearly goals for the company, my team, and for my own personal progress.

You are probably very familiar with old approaches to goal setting that have been around for years, such as SMART goals. Every year, the company I worked for would have me fill out my yearly objectives, define several goals they would like me to work on, and then ask me to create a couple of personal goals. I followed the process and defined my goals following the prescribed format. Then, before the end of the year, I was expected to update my goals, mark their status of completion, and add some description of what took place.

This has been my approach to setting goals for as long as I can remember. Over the years, I had some good managers who would follow up and ask how I was doing on my goals, which provided a level of accountability, and they would ask me to update my progress. But did any of these goals inspire me or motivate me to do amazing things? That is a big fat "NO." It was more of an exercise in fulfilling a requirement of employment.

The traditional way you set goals is to find an attainable goal that seems doable within a certain window of time and then define it using an approach like SMART. Using a very linear approach, you would take one step at a time and follow through on your goals. This approach works, and it works great, which is why it has been taught for so many years.

The approach to attaining these goals is straightforward, and you have often already accomplished a similar goal in the past. Because it's so familiar to both your mind and body, the memory and belief on how to do it are within you, and you can achieve it fairly easily.

At times, I have set some incredibly challenging goals, but because of how the corporate world is set up and how they structure your year-end review, it has the effect of discouraging people from setting anything outlandish or stretched. That is because who wants to fail their year-end review? Everyone is trying to look good to get their next raise or bonus, so no one wants to set any goals that require them to get out of their comfort zone and do something incredible.

Suppose you always set your goals and intentions for your future with the same level of thinking, looking to past experiences to determine how you achieved previous goals and using the same methods, techniques, and systems you have always used. What do you suppose your future will look like?

For most of my career, I followed the prescribed path until I found something that ignited my life.

What if there was something that could boost your performance and get you where you wanted to be ten times faster?

What if you wanted to achieve ten times or 100 times more than you used to accomplish? Now, what do you do?

This is where dreaming big and using your imagination to create and set a seemingly impossible goal comes in. Over the last few years, much research has been done on setting highly challenging or seemingly unattainable goals.

Researchers have found that setting highly difficult goals can lead people to higher performance levels. This pushes them to think more creatively and find innovative solutions. Because the goal is highly challenging, it can unify and motivate teams and organizations.

An example of this type of goal could be doing something you have never done before, like starting your own business or writing your very first book. If you are a business owner and running a business, double your sales this year or double your sales in a shorter time frame than before, say six months or even in three months rather than a year. I have seen some people do nearly impossible things like double and triple their income in just a few months, setting "impossible" goals.

How is attaining a highly challenging goal different from a regular achievable one?

Since the highly challenging goal initially feels impossible, it will require a different approach to attain than you have done in the past. It will require you to approach the goal with a new level of thinking and being. Doing the impossible will require you to think creatively about the solution, and you may have to do something you have never done before. Rather than thinking about how you approached it from the past, there will be no history to help you achieve it, but you will have to approach it from the future.

It is time to start dreaming big and setting big, seemingly impossible goals. They will push you out of your current comfort zone. Research shows that when we set bigger goals that stretch us, we are more motivated. The sheer size of them can keep you more committed to achieving them and keep you more focused and energized over the long term.

Action

If you want to see a greater transformation in your life, it's time to start dreaming bigger.

- Write down one goal in each of The Four Pillars (Vitality, Insight, Harmony, and Purpose) that would radically transform your life.

There is additional information on how to design your future self and start "Dreaming the Impossible." Go to: e3blueprint.com/bookbonus to get more details.

MOVING ACROSS THE GAP

> *"To change is to think greater than your environment. To think greater than the circumstances in your life, to think greater than the conditions in your world. And to keep thinking and feeling the same way—independent of the conditions in your outer environment—is how you close the gap between your future and your present."*
> **– Dr. Joe Dispenza**

Once you start dreaming and imagining the future you would like to have, you'll start to see a gap between where you are and where you want to be. Looking out into the future exercises your imagination, and I hope you're dreaming big. But the bigger the dream, the bigger the gap you will see. The gap is the unknown and uncharted territory between the present and the future.

This gap can sometimes feel so large and vast that it may feel so incredibly overwhelming that you can't even begin. Many have attempted to cross over this unknown territory and have failed time and time again to return to what they know habitually as their present self. They return to an area that feels safe and easy, known as their "comfort zone."

Barely returning to safety after your last failed attempt, you might start assessing what went wrong and make adjustments for your next attempt. However, if you have tried and tried again, you might be like most people and start to reassess your hopes and dreams. You may end up turning them down a notch or two or end up canceling them altogether.

When you lose hope for a better future, this is where depression and despair set in, and if you stay in this place too long, it can have terrible effects on all the pillars of your life. The beautiful thing about humanity is that we have this innate ability to rise up after disaster and help each other overcome adversity.

Before I learned all of these concepts and after many failed attempts at living the life I wanted, I found myself in a dark place I call the "pit." A dark pit of despair. Some may think it is a bad place to be in, but it was in this place that I felt there was nowhere to go but up. In this place, great inspiration came to me to rebuild my life, to stop focusing on what I have or what everyone else has, and to focus on who I can become. Because of that place, I started a journey of self-discovery and searching for ways to recreate my life in the best possible way.

Because of that experience, I gained a new perspective and could focus on creating the life I wanted. I could see the gap of the unknown, not as things that I didn't know how to do or were impossible to figure out, but as a gap between my present self and my future self.

Who do I have to become to attain my goal?

It's not so much about how to attain my goal but about becoming the future version of myself who has already attained it. This is a new way of thinking about your dreams and goals.

Start by seeing your future self as already having reached and fulfilled all your dreams and goals. See your future as having experienced everything it took to get there. You should notice that since your future version of yourself is much different from the version of yourself today, there should be a noticeable difference between who you are today and the future version of yourself when you have achieved your goals.

To become the future version of yourself that you see, you will begin the transformation process of closing the gap between who you are today and who you are in the future. The bigger and more audacious the goal, the greater the transformation that will have to occur.

Action

Take a few minutes and journal about the following questions:

- What new choices and decisions must be made to be this future version of you?
- What must be learned to expand you mentally and spiritually?
- What new habits must be practiced to elevate you to the next level of being?

Note: The wording on the previous questions. The wording used is "must." Asking your subconscious mind the right questions will result in better answers.

FOCUSING ON THE GAIN

> *"Life is like riding a bicycle. To keep your balance, you must keep moving."*
> **– Albert Einstein**

I will put a different spin on the future self-concept because if not done correctly, it can lead to frustration. For three decades, I chased this elusive dream of being the best. It started early on as a small boy because I had two older and bigger brothers who were stronger and more athletic than I was, and because of that, my dad would take my brothers out and train them in sports like tennis, racquetball, golf, snow skiing, and water skiing, to name a few.

When I got old enough for my turn to learn, Dad's patience had worn a little thin. Even though I was given an opportunity to learn the same sports as my older brothers, I felt I didn't get the same level of time and energy invested into my training as my brothers. My dad loved to play, so he liked to play with those who gave him the greatest competitive challenge, and that was certainly not me.

I remember many golfing trips where I was being yelled at for hitting the ball into the woods, never to be found, or if I duffed a shot a few feet ahead, he would tell me to hurry up and run up there and hit it because we didn't want to delay those behind us. By no means was my father a bad man. He was a great man and gave me tons of opportunities as a child, but it was these experiences that created some faulty programming and where I formulated a belief in myself that I wasn't good enough. I didn't discover this until years later when I was literally having a nervous breakdown, and a good friend of mine helped me discover this faulty program.

For years, I chased every sport that my brothers had to try to be the best. They tried out for the basketball, football, and track teams, and then I would do the same. For each sport I tried, I would at least stick it out for a season to see if I would like it or not, and most often, I found myself moving on until I found wrestling. I finally found a sport I felt I could excel at, and I did for the most part. I ended up lettering in wrestling three years in a row in high school but never reached the level of success my brothers did in their wrestling careers.

Both brothers played a few musical instruments; my oldest played in the band and the choir, and my other brother was in the jazz band. I attempted piano, guitar, and saxophone and quit all of them after being laughed at and mocked when playing a song at a family gathering. I struggled to keep rhythm, and I guess that is what made everyone laugh so hard.

One thing I did well was my academics. I graduated from high school as a salutatorian, and to rank second highest in my graduating class wasn't too bad. As a young man, it might have made my head swell a little bit. However, when I enrolled in Electrical Engineering at college, I found out there were many people who were way smarter than I was. Everyone seemed to learn faster, finish their homework faster, and do better on every exam. I had to work extremely hard to compete and keep my grades up.

Once I graduated, I found a job at Novell, one of the area's biggest technology companies. It so happened that both my brothers were working there too. Let's stop here for a minute: back then, I would have never recognized the subconscious programming that led me to the same company as my brothers. I started my career there in the same department that they did, and for the next twenty years, my subconscious programming pushed me to be the best.

I already had a habit of looking into the future and envisioning myself as one of the top developers and architects the company employed. Early on in my career, I worked around the clock, and I innovated and created some very cool technologies. Because of that work, I hold several patents, and my work ethic drove me to become a leader of multiple teams where we delivered world-class software products to some of the top companies in the world.

The elusive dream of being the best and good enough just never seemed to get close because there was always someone who was just a bit smarter or had the right answers that would make it seem like I would never attain that status as the best.

It wasn't until one day that a good friend of mine helped me uncover the real reason behind this drive to succeed, which changed my entire perspective on life.

For the past thirty years, I have been striving and working just to feel good enough, not to myself but to my father and brothers. When I finally realized this truth, everything began to unravel, and the great house of cards I had been building just tumbled down. This realization of why I was pushing myself so hard came well before my wife passed away, so I didn't hit rock bottom until a few years after her death.

I don't think I am alone in not feeling good enough. Jamie Kern Lima released a book called *Worthy* to help people embrace their self-worth and overcome feelings of inadequacy. It instantly became a *New York Times* bestseller. My wife, Janice, and I attended the book launch and watched as millions of copies were sold in a single day. There are a lot of people on this planet who do not feel adequate about themselves.

For most of my life, I focused on becoming the ideal version of success, which seemed to move farther away. I always compared myself to others who were more successful than me and to others who had more than myself. This thinking only brought suffering and pain. It only brought thoughts of inadequacy and feelings of not being good enough.

In *The Happiness Advantage*, Shawn Achor shares the concept of "moving the goalpost," which refers to how people continuously shift their definition of success, making it harder to achieve happiness. In his book, Achor explains that many people, after reaching a goal, immediately move the goalpost farther by setting new, often unattainable targets. This behavior prevents them from ever feeling satisfied or happy because they never take the time to appreciate their accomplishments.

Achor argues that instead of continually raising the bar, it's essential to celebrate success and find happiness in the present. Focusing on positive habits and acknowledging your achievements can improve your well-being and productivity without chasing an ever-moving target. This idea is central to the book's overall message that success doesn't lead to happiness; rather, cultivating happiness can lead to greater success.

The key point of sharing my story was that I experienced tremendous amounts of unhappiness and even years of depression because the goalpost was always moving. I was always focused on becoming this ideal engineer that could never be attained because the definition of success kept changing. I failed to take the time to celebrate how far I had come along my journey, but I was only looking for the next milestone of achievement.

In the previous chapters, we focused on creating our future selves and setting these incredible goals, which can create a massive gap between who we are today and who we want to become. If your focus is constantly on the gap or the ideal of who you want to become, much like I did in my life, it may bring anxiety and unhappiness.

Although I wanted to strive to become this new future version of myself, my focus was always on the ideal that was forever changing and eluding me. It was like chasing the horizon.

Throughout life, we are forever changing in one direction or another, and change is inevitable. When you focus on improving your life, change will occur, causing you to reassess your ideal future self. If you are waiting to declare victory and feel all the emotions that success brings, you will never reach that "pot of gold" at the end of the rainbow.

The Gain is the Solution

Can you see the dilemma?

I just had you focus on creating a big, bright future. But with it comes "the gap," that space or void between who you are in the present and the ideal future self you want to create. Too much focus on "the gap" is the reason I had so much anxiety and felt like I was never good enough.

The solution to this dilemma is to know where you're placing your focus. You want to be able to move across the gap without always focusing on your shortcomings and what you lack. You will need to stop focusing on "the gap," but you will need to focus on "the gain."

What is "the gain?"

It is the measurement of your past to the present. You calculate and measure your gain by looking back and reviewing your progress over time. This is looking back with a new perspective. You are looking back at your past to use it as a tool. You are looking at the lessons you have learned and the progress you have made up to now.

The emphasis on focusing on your future self was to get motivated and excited about the future, to create a massive drive and passion to move forward. You can't go anywhere in life before you have a destination to navigate to; otherwise, you will go nowhere but in circles.

Now that you have this gap to close, it is only natural that your thoughts will gravitate to what you are lacking. The future that you envision will include things that others already have, and this will cause you to want to compare your life with theirs, which will only bring anxiety and suffering to yourself.

This is an important mind shift: life is not a race with everyone else to see who can accumulate the most stuff before we die. It's unimportant to anyone else how far or fast you have gone. The very second you stop comparing yourself to others, your suffering can end, and happiness can start.

Dan Sullivan wrote an entire book on this topic called *The Gap and The Gain*, The book argues that living in "the Gap" leads to feelings of frustration, inadequacy, and failure, while living in "the Gain" fosters gratitude, satisfaction, and motivation. By shifting your mindset to appreciate how far you've come rather than focusing on how far you still want to go, you will achieve greater happiness, productivity, and long-term success.

I started to practice looking for the gain with my team of engineers daily and weekly, and the results were remarkable. There was a greater level of motivation and contribution among the engineers. Focusing on our "wins" really helped boost the morale of the team and each member's overall level of fulfillment.

Adding this as a weekly and monthly habit has boosted my motivation toward my future goals and ambitions. The process of focusing on "the gain" is focusing on your progress; we are all learning something, and we are all changing from day to day. When you get in the habit of seeing the small wins in your life and your progress, it will bring about greater happiness. You will experience feelings of gratitude for what you have experienced, and as a result, you will feel greater levels of fulfillment and joy.

Focusing on the gain will give you that extra energy boost when things are hard. When setting out to become a new version of yourself and achieving impossible goals, roadblocks big and small will show up and try to deter you on your way, but putting into practice a daily, weekly, and monthly focus of looking back and seeing how far you have come along the way will give you a whole new perspective and mindset.

Looking for the "wins" in your life will begin to train your brain to see the small things making a big difference in your life and those around you. The more you practice seeing the small "wins" in your life, the more apparent it will be that success is not measured by ideals but by progress. Focusing on the gains will help you cultivate gratitude for even the small wins, leading to greater mental well-being.

When you focus on your improvements rather than your comparisons to others, your confidence will increase. By staying in "the gain," you will experience greater motivation and happiness, with greater gains and opportunities on the way.

Focusing on "the gain" will allow you to create the life you dreamed of.

Action

Take a few minutes to journal:

- Look back over the last year and ask yourself, "What wins, accomplishments, achievements have I had over this year?"

HARNESSING YOUR CREATIVE FORCE

> *"The quantum field responds not to what we want; it responds to who we are being."*
> – Dr. Joe Dispenza

Have you ever been at a party, and someone walks into the room, and you feel this negative energy? It might feel like all the energy drained out of the room. When I was taking martial arts with my two oldest children several years back, our sensei would call that person an "energy vampire." A person that sucks the energy right out of you. You may know someone who can drain you emotionally and energetically.

I want you to recognize that energy not only in others but also in yourself. One key principle in manifesting anything in your life is to use positive energy to create the desired outcomes. On the other hand, negative energy will bring results that you may not desire.

Harnessing Your Creative Force

Your thoughts and emotions are, in essence, the creative energy that you are sending out into the universe. To move toward the future version of yourself, you must start to feel the emotions your future self will be experiencing. The closer you are to having and experiencing the same level of emotions as your future self, the greater the probability of manifesting your dreams becomes.

This is one of the most difficult things you will have in imagining your future because it is extremely hard to imagine the feelings of an experience if you have never experienced it before. This is where people have the greatest disconnect between their present and future selves. It is hard to force your brain and body to believe something that it doesn't believe to be true. More often than not, you will have a set of programs running in your subconscious telling you that what you want to do is truly impossible, and this faulty programming will try to convince you that if you try, you will fail, so why try? Give up now.

Let's overcome this programming by tricking it into believing your future is possible. You must use higher emotions your brain and body can believe in and accept. These emotions are love, gratitude, and joy. They are emotions that will generate higher-frequency energy waves.

Can you be grateful that the future you are imagining is happening for you? Can you feel love for those around you in the future? Can you feel the joy of an experience?

Since you have not had the experience in the future and you are still determining what to expect, using emotions like gratitude is something you can feel and expect to feel if you were to succeed at your desired goal.

One of my first coaches and mentors had me make a list of affirmations that he wanted me to declare to myself, so he had me stand up, look in the mirror, and say these words with some energy that would make anyone feel amazing. I could believe some of the affirmations and feel their energy when I declared them out loud, but others felt a bit disjointed, or in other words, I felt no connection to the words. My brain and body had no experience with these words, so I wouldn't believe them no matter how many times I tried to repeat the sentence.

I later learned a simple technique to trick the brain. Use gratitude with the words I am trying to emulate. Adding "I am grateful for" in front of any sentence made it feel truer. It became more believable to my subconscious mind and easier to accept. Also, journaling how grateful I am for accomplishing my goals helped to elicit positive emotions about my future self.

The more you practice envisioning your future self and feeling the emotions of being grateful and happy that you have achieved your future experience, the closer you will get to feeling what it might feel like when arriving at being your future self.

Using these emotions will help you narrow the gap, and it will become easier for your mind and body to accept this new possibility you envisioned for yourself. Your conscious mind will become more aware of things happening in your present, and the "lens" you are filtering the world with will begin to gather evidence that the things you are saying and dreaming about can come true. And what may have seemed impossible in the past will become possible.

Letting Go

A few years ago, I went on one of the longest hikes I had ever been on. I met a group of friends at 6 a.m. at the trailhead, and we began our way up to one of the highest peaks in the area. I wouldn't consider myself an avid hiker, but some group members were very seasoned. I packed a small backpack with just the essentials: an extra pair of socks, a light jacket, some first-aid materials, sunscreen, food for lunch, snacks, and water. I slid the pack's straps over my shoulders, and we began our fourteen-hour hike.

When you throw a small pack on your back that weighs less than thirty pounds, it's quite light at first and doesn't seem to bother you, but over time, the weight of that pack began to wear on my shoulders and feel a bit heavy. The longer we hiked and the more tired I got, the heavier it got until finally, when we reached the bottom later that evening, it felt good to remove the pack and return it to the trunk of my car.

Negative emotions can be very much like that pack. At first, they can be very light and easy to tote around with you, but if you hold on to them over time, they will get heavy and weigh you down. The problem is that we don't pack around one or two; we usually have many negative emotions we are lugging around with us most of the time.

When we fail to release negative emotions, they manifest as stress and disease in the body. These emotions can be triggered often and hamper progress, even preventing us from making good decisions and acting toward becoming the future self that we dream of.

Our state of being is very much the emotions we carry and display daily, so releasing and letting go of negative emotions is an important step in allowing yourself to become the future self you desire.

Once you can let go, you will be free. You will be lighter than ever before and one step closer to becoming your future self.

Action:

Take a few minutes to journal:

- How grateful you must be to have reached your goal and achieved this new level of success.

Let go of those negative emotions by going to e3blueprint.com/bookbonus, where you will learn and practice some "let go" techniques to free yourself from negative emotions.

STEPPING FORWARD WITH FAITH

> *"What the mind can conceive and believe, it can achieve."*
> **– Napoleon Hill**

Sooner or later, there will come a point where you must decide to go all-in on your dreams and desires. This is called the "point of no return" when a decision is made, and there is no going back.

You've probably heard the term "burning your boats" coined from stories like Alexander the Great's invasion of Persia. Upon landing his army on Persian shores, he ordered his men to burn their ships, ensuring that there would be no retreat. His troops then had no choice but to march forward and conquer the Persian Empire.

Earlier, I mentioned Neo. In the movie *The Matrix*, he was given the choice to take the red or blue pill. The red pill would reveal the truth of the world, showing Neo the reality of the Matrix—a simulation controlling humanity—while the blue pill would allow him to return to his normal life, oblivious to the truth. By choosing the red pill, Neo crossed the threshold into a reality that forever changed him.

At some point in your journey into the unknown, you must decide whether to take a leap of faith and act toward becoming your future self or stay stuck in your habitual past. It's up to you.

The choice is now yours. What will it be, the red pill or the blue pill?

A New Level of Mind

Attempting to attain seemingly impossible goals and crossing the gap of the unknown will require you to do things differently. Albert Einstein stated, "We cannot solve our problems with the same thinking we used when we created them." It suggests that to achieve nearly impossible goals, you must adopt a mindset entirely different from the one you had when you set those goals. Achieving the extraordinary requires a transformation of thought—a leap to a new level of consciousness or faith.

Including faith in creating your future self will help you break free from old mindsets that have kept you imprisoned and tied to past limitations. It will give you the confidence to embrace new, uncharted possibilities.

Your old programming and mindsets are often rooted in fear, doubt, and limitations that prevent you from envisioning your desired future. However, adding faith will allow you to believe in something beyond what you have experienced. **With a new level of thinking, you trust that new possibilities can be accessed through belief and action, even when they don't seem apparent.**

Facing the Unknown

The older we get, the harder it is to leave our "comfort zone," that place that is easy and known. When you set out to create a new version of yourself, you are stepping into the unknown, and it can cause you to feel uncertain and overwhelmed. I couldn't count how often I have ventured out to try something new, only to retreat to what I know and what allows me to sleep well at night.

Your old subconscious programming wants to cling to the known and comfortable, but with the added power of faith, it allows you to take steps into the unknown with trust.

Doubts and fears will still arise, but faith will give you the courage to let go of any guaranteed outcomes and take brave action steps out of your comfort zone into the unknown. It will shift your focus from fear and anxiety of the unknown to excitement about what's possible.

The Future Is Not Equal to the Past

Your old programming limits you to living your life in the past, and it causes you to think that you are only capable of doing what you have always done. It is often rigid and based on past failures, missed opportunities, or perceived weaknesses. And the minute you decide to take a stand and move forward into the future, your old programming will trigger and let you know that it was much safer where you were before. Then the retreat occurs back into the zone of comfort and ease. Or perhaps it's not a comfort zone but one that is known.

Faith allows you to transcend and transform into something that will allow you to move forward. Adding faith into the equation will help reinforce the idea that your past does not define your future. You will begin to see yourself not as a product of the past but as a creator of your future. A believing mindset encourages you to believe in bigger possibilities and trust that you can grow into them, even if your current reality doesn't reflect them yet.

A new mindset around faith invites flexibility in thinking because it opens the door to hope and belief in new outcomes. It will lead to newly sparked creativity and innovation, allowing you to think beyond the boundaries of your past and explore solutions not previously considered.

As the creator of your future, you will approach life with **"life happens for me"** and **"what could be"** rather than "life happens to me" and "what has been."

Belief in God

I am not here to tell you what to believe or how to believe, but each person ought to be fully respected in what they do believe. When you add your faith in a higher power, a transformative power exists that would not be there otherwise. It's entirely up to you to believe in God, the universe, the quantum field, or some external power. Adding a belief in a higher power will give you added strength to transform and achieve things that seem impossible.

Research has shown that belief in God or a higher power is linked to numerous positive psychological, emotional, and social outcomes. It provides a sense of meaning, helps you cope with adversity, fosters resilience, and can even contribute to better physical health. Having a belief in God has helped me face some of the most difficult and challenging circumstances that life can throw at a person, with the suicide of my best friend, the death of my three-year-old daughter, and the sudden death of my wife, Amy, as well as divorce, remarriage, and the challenges of blending families. It has allowed me to turn from a victim mentality of "why me" to a creator of my life and a mindset of "life happens for me" and "what can I make life be."

Being a creator of your life doesn't mean bad things won't happen to you, but it means that you will take control of what you think and how you respond to what life presents. One significant observation of life along our journey of learning to be creators is that we may not be able to control all our circumstances, but we do have the ability to bless and enhance the lives of others.

Faith isn't just about belief; it's about embodying a mindset willing to step beyond the known and into the realm of possibility. By incorporating faith into the process of creating your future self, you create a mental and emotional foundation that supports new ways of thinking, acting, and being. Faith empowers you to let go of old mindsets tied to past limitations and opens the space for the new future you're creating.

CLOSING THE LOOP
FROM VISION TO REALITY

> *"Life is never made unbearable by circumstances, but only by lack of meaning and purpose."*
> **– Viktor Frankl**

Along the journey of reinventing my life and learning how to be a creator of my reality, I realized how critically important the Envision phase is in the creation process. I was stuck for nearly three decades in depression with no end in sight until I learned how to dream and imagine again. When I finally learned to stop focusing on the mistakes of the past that generated the negative emotions of guilt and shame and started seeing them as life lessons, everything shifted. It was then that I could stop looking backward with regret and forward with hope and optimism. I could start seeing a new version of the person I could become.

Feelings of happiness, joy, and love started to flow throughout my body, and miracles started appearing in my life as I practiced envisioning a brighter and bigger future. Take a moment to reflect on the transformative power of dreaming and imagining a compelling future.

This Envision phase is about defining your future, shifting your mindset, and aligning your energy, thoughts, and actions toward the future you wish to create. Envisioning is an act of creation. All things, big or small, must go through the process of spiritual or mental creation before they can be manifested in reality, and it is through this act that the foundation of your future is built.

Do not let your circumstances constrict your ability to envision a powerful future. Over time, while practicing and going through the envisioning phase, how you see your current reality will drastically change. A brighter, happier reality will start to appear.

I hope you look beyond what seems possible today and start believing in the transformative potential and great power that lies within you. Take time daily to connect with your future self, and allow yourself to be pulled forward with purpose, clarity, and excitement. Each vision you craft and each step you take brings you closer to becoming the person you aspire to be.

From Vision to Reality

Hold fast to the lessons learned in this phase: the importance of hope, the strength of imagination, and the conviction that you are the creator of your destiny. With this clarity of vision, you now stand at the gateway to a future full of possibility and purpose. The future is waiting for you to step into it—boldly, intentionally, and with unwavering faith.

Embrace this next step in your journey. Your future is already unfolding, and with every moment, you are becoming the person you were meant to be.

CONCLUSION

> "It is not the critic who counts; not the man who points out how the strong man stumbles, or where the doer of deeds could have done them better. The credit belongs to the man who is actually in the arena, whose face is marred by dust and sweat and blood; who strives valiantly; who errs, who comes short again and again, because there is no effort without error and shortcoming; but who does actually strive to do the deeds; who knows great enthusiasms, the great devotions; who spends himself in a worthy cause; who at the best knows in the end the triumph of high achievement, and who at the worst, if he fails, at least fails while daring greatly, so that his place shall never be with those cold and timid souls who neither know victory nor defeat."
> – Theodore Roosevelt

Over the last several years, I have poured my time and attention into learning from the best and brightest in the world. I believe that God instills truth into all of us and wants us to influence everyone in the world positively. Everyone is unique in mind and spirit, and some lessons can be learned from each other.

Conclusion

For some, the path I have walked in life might look easy, and to others, it might be unbearably hard. The degree of difficulty does not matter, but what you learn along your journey matters because how you respond to life and the message you share from your heart will bless, inspire, and lift those around you.

I share with you the concepts I have discovered and learned as The Creation Formula because I know they can be transformative to your life as they have been for mine. If you just put into practice the three "E's" of living—Expand, Elevate, and Envision—you will start to see a transformation occur daily in your life. And not only will you see it in your life but also in the lives of those within your circle of influence and proximity.

Because of the shift in your energy, your influence will be seen and felt, and without a word, you will begin a transformative change in your family and the lives around you. I noticed this shift in my own life and my children's lives. When I improved, they improved. With improvement in one area, all the pillars of my life improved.

Practicing the principles of The Creation Formula empowers you to reclaim control over your life, allowing you to be intentional with the design of your future that you desire. It will elevate you to a new level of purposeful living. By engaging in the work of transformation, you not only bless your own life but also positively impact the lives of others. They become beneficiaries of the transformation you undertake.

As I sat at my father's funeral, I reflected on how one man could impact so many. He profoundly affected my life and influenced me to live a good life. He had over 100 direct descendants, including children, grandchildren, and great-grandchildren. And then many other relatives, friends, and neighbors were influenced by this great man. I am sure there were hundreds or even thousands over his lifetime that he was able to influence. His life's effect will continue to live on through future generations.

Your life is meaningful, and what you decide to do from this point forward can have a significant impact and influence, for good or bad. You can be like the rising tide lifting all that rests on its surface. So let this be the time for you to rise and bless the lives of all those around you.

Don't let your past trap you into being a victim of life. Don't let your circumstances imprison you for a life that can't change. Your view of the world is just a series of assumptions and expectations learned from birth—you have the power within you to change it all.

Be a Creator, not a victim.
Be a Creator of your health.
Be the Creator of your being.
Be the Creator of your relationships.
Be the Creator of your wealth.

Be the creator God intended you to be by expanding your mind and spirit, elevating your state of being, and envisioning a bright, beautiful future.

REFERENCES

Achor, Shawn. *The Happiness Advantage: The Seven Principles of Positive Psychology That Fuel Success and Performance at Work*. Crown, 2010.

Bergland, Christopher. "The Brain Mechanics of Rumination and Repetitive Thinking." *Psychology Today*, 1 August 2015, https://www.psychologytoday.com/us/blog/the-athletes-way/201508/the-brain-mechanics-rumination-and-repetitive-thinking. Accessed 12 July 2024.

"The CBT Model of Emotions." *Cognitive Behavioral Therapy Los Angeles*, https://cogbtherapy.com/cbt-model-of-emotions. Accessed 12 July 2024.

Clear, James. *Atomic Habits: An Easy & Proven Way to Build Good Habits & Break Bad Ones*. Penguin Publishing Group, 2018.

Collins, James Charles, and Jerry I. Porras. *Built to Last: Successful Habits of Visionary Companies*. HarperCollins, 2004. Accessed 18 August 2024.

Dispenza, Joe. *Breaking The Habit of Being Yourself: How to Lose Your Mind and Create a New One*. Hay House, 2013.

Elkrief, Noah. *A Guide to the Present Moment: How to Stop Believing the Thoughts that Keep You from Feeling Free, Whole, and Happy*. Noah Elkrief, 2012.

Elrod, Hal. *The Miracle Morning (Updated and Expanded Edition): The Not-So-Obvious Secret Guaranteed to Transform Your Life (Before 8AM)*. BenBella Books, 2023.

Frankl, Viktor E. *Man's Search For Meaning*. Pocket Books, 1985.

Hardy, Benjamin. *Be Your Future Self Now: The Science of Intentional Transformation*. Hay House, 2022.

Katie, Byron, and Stephen Mitchell. *Loving What Is*. Three Rivers Press, 2003.

Khatri, Minesh. "ACT Therapy: What It Is and How It Can Benefit Your Mental Health." *WebMD*, 14 May 2023, https://www.webmd.com/mental-health/what-is-acceptance-and-commitment-therapy. Accessed 12 July 2024.

Leaf, Caroline, and Leaf. *Switch On Your Brain: The Key to Peak Happiness, Thinking, and Health*. Baker Publishing Group, 2015.

Locke, EA, and GP Latham. *Building a Practically Useful Theory of Goal Setting and Task Motivation*,

References

https://med.stanford.edu/content/dam/sm/s-spire/documents/PD.locke-and-latham-retrospective_Paper.pdf. Accessed 18 August 2024.

McCraty, Rollin. "The Energetic Heart: Bioelectromagnetic Communication Within and Between People." *HeartMath Institute*, https://www.heartmath.org/research/research-library/energetics/energetic-heart-bioelectromagnetic-communication-within-and-between-people/. Accessed 3 August 2024.

Niels Bohr. "On the Constitution of Atoms and Molecules." *Philosophical Magazine*, vol. 26, 1913, pp. 1-24. https://www.tandfonline.com/doi/abs/10.1080/14786441308634955.

NLP Techniques, 85+ Free Techniques, Worldwide 1:1 Training, https://www.nlp-techniques.org/. Accessed 21 September 2024.

Robbins, Anthony. *Awaken the Giant Within: How to Take Immediate Control of Your Mental, Emotional, Physical and Financial Destiny*. Pocket, 2001.

Robbins, Tony. *Unleash the Power Within: Personal Coaching from Anthony Robbins That Will Transform Your Life!* Simon & Schuster Audio/Nightingale-Conant, 2012.

Sullivan, Dan, and Dr. Benjamin Hardy. *The Gap and The Gain: The High Achievers' Guide to Happiness, Confidence, and Success*. Hay House, 2021.

Sullivan, Dan, and Dr. Benjamin Hardy. *10x Is Easier Than 2x: How World-Class Entrepreneurs Achieve More by Doing Less*. Hay House, 2023.

Tolle, Eckhart. *The power of now*. Namaste Pub., 2004.

"Wide-Angle Lens vs. Telephoto Lens: Understanding the Difference - 2024." *MasterClass*, 7 June 2021, https://www.masterclass.com/articles/wide-angle-lens-vs-telephoto-lens-understanding-the-difference#when-to-use-a-telephoto-lens. Accessed 12 July 2024.

ABOUT THE AUTHOR

Nathan B. Jensen is a certified hypnotherapist, high-performance coach, NLP practitioner, and meditation instructor with a deep passion for personal development, neuroscience, and quantum theory. As a contributor to the best-selling book *The Wealth Code*, Nathan brings a wealth of knowledge and experience to the personal growth space. Over the past few years, he has read over 250 books and completed training with some of the most respected names in the industry, including Tony Robbins, Brendon Burchard, Jack Canfield, and Dr. Joe Dispenza.

In his latest work, *In Search of The Creation Formula*, Nathan combines his vast knowledge and personal experiences to offer readers a practical guide to transforming their lives. His approach integrates neuroscience, NLP, and spiritual principles, helping individuals overcome limiting beliefs and design their future with clarity and intention.

With more than two decades of experience leading and mentoring technical teams, Nathan's ability to merge technical expertise with personal growth makes him a sought-after coach and mentor.

In his spare time, Nathan enjoys spending time with his wife, seven children, and nine grandchildren. He is committed to continuous self-improvement and is passionate about fitness, learning, and exploring the latest in neuroscience. Nathan resides in Utah and can be reached at nathan@e3blueprint.com for speaking, coaching, and consulting opportunities.

www.ingramcontent.com/pod-product-compliance
Lightning Source LLC
Chambersburg PA
CBHW050634160426
43194CB00010B/1666